SEGOVIA CATHEDRAL

P9-CAX-980

Editor in chief: Vicente Pastor

Design: V. Pastor and J. Alegre

Photographs: Norberto, Imagen M.A.S. (pages 14, 44, 47 and 52) and Manuel Martín (pages 42, 68-69, 77 and 80d)

This book was written with the collaboration of the Chapter of Segovia Cathedral.

© *Text:* José Antonio Ruiz Hernando

© EDILESA
General Sanjurjo, 7 - 24001 León, Spain
Telephone: (987) 22 10 66

1st Edition - 1995

I.S.B.N.: 84-8012-076-2
Depósito Legal: LE-212-1995
Printed in Spain. Impreso en España

All rights reserved:
No part of this publication may be reproduced, stored in a retrieval system, or transmitted in any form or by any means, electronic, mechanical photocopying, recording, or otherwise, without the prior permission of the publishers.

SEGOVIA CATHEDRAL

Text by:

JOSÉ ANTONIO RUIZ HERNANDO

Photographs by

NORBERTO

English Translation:

GORDON KEITCH

Edilesa

CONTENTS

SEGOVIA CATHEDRAL. Groundplan

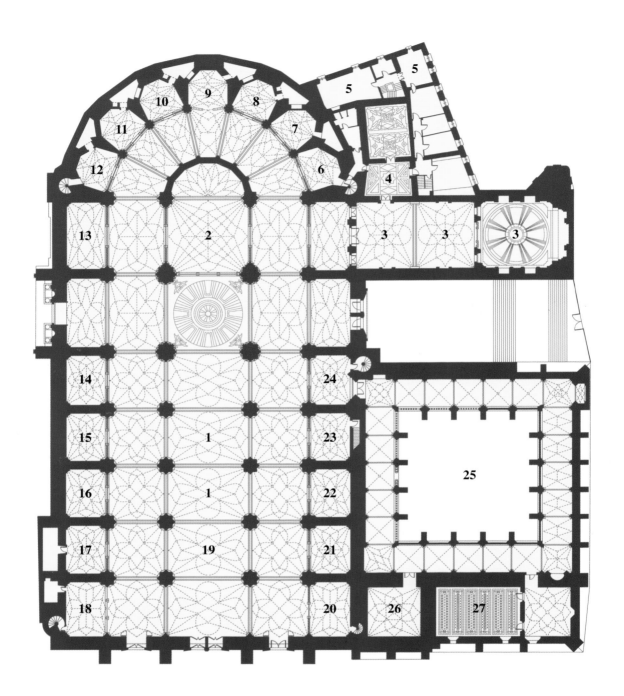

1. Choir
2. Chancel
3. Chapel of the Tabernacle
4. Sacristy
5. Archives
6. St Peter's Chapel
7. St Ildefonsus's Chapel
8. St Geroteo's Chapel
9. St Frutos's Chapel

10. St Anthony's Chapel
11. Chapel of Our Lady of the Rosary
12. St Joseph's Chapel
13. St Antón's Chapel
14. Chapel of the *Pietà*
15. St Andrew's Chapel
16. Chapel of St Cosmas and St Damian
17. St Gregory's Chapel
18. Chapel of the Conception

19. Chapel of the Retrochoir
20. St Blasius's Chapel
21. Chapel of the Taking Down
22. St Barbara's Chapel
23. St James's Chapel
24. Chapel of the Christ of Solace
25. Cloister
26. St Catherine's Chapel
27. Chapter-house

Groundplan by and through the courtesy of Merino de Cáceres.

INTRODUCTION

Segovia, in the centre of Spain, is a beautiful model of medieval town planning; the tangible reality of the backgrounds of so many Gothic paintings showing the houses huddled together on the hillside and the cathedral tower standing graceful over them. The traveller who approaches Segovia by the Ávila or Valladolid road sees the bulk of the cathedral from a long way off over the golden cornfields, and little by little is offered the towers and roofs, and then the city wall over the green valley.

The cathedral is the fitting high point of the city's religious architecture and, we could even say, of all its architecture. Only the church of the *Colegio de la Compañía*, begun some years later and completed much earlier, is worthy of note and no mean amount is to be learnt by comparing the two buildings in order to see just how closely the plans drawn in 1524 were kept to as time and fashion passed. When it was finished, right at the end of the 17th Century, Segovia had lost the importance it had once known, its houses had long since taken up all the available space and the townsfolk were beginning to notice a decadence that was to last into the present century. From the artistic point of view, the building twelve kilometres away of *La Granja de San Ildefonso* for Philip V, the first Borbón (Spanish Bourbon) monarch, was to make itself felt, though on a small scale, in Segovia and especially in the cathedral, where the affability of the people was complemented by the courtesy of the Court.

The great volume of the cathedral, its mighty tower and the roundness of the dome have caught the imagination of painters - Segovia is a city to paint - and, naturally, writers, who have lavished praise on it, among whom are Pío Baroja, Azorín, Ramón Gómez de la Serna, Ortega y Gasset, etc., whom we may quote:

On the left, in the distance, sails Segovia cathedral on a sea of golden wheat, like a great mystic liner, overshadowing the rest of the buildings with its girth. At this time of day it takes on an olive hue, and an optical illusion makes it seem to cut a path through the golden corn with its apse. Between its flying buttresses blue cut-outs of sky show as between the stays and shrouds of a ship.

J. Ortega y Gasset
Notas de Vago Estío. *El Espectador V* (1926)

The tower of the cathedral stood over it with class, with a stiffness so perpendicular to the ground, with such erect height, like a great flagstone stood on its end, amazing anyone who looked up from its feet.

R. Gómez de la Serna
The Secret of the Aqueduct

Segovia cathedral, in the centre of the city, leaves the rest of the buildings flat, although their relationship was once very different because of the resettlement.

Preceding pages:

Buttresses.
Only an expert could date them in the 17th Century, when the east end was finished.

The cathedral from the walls of the Carmelites' garden. In the foreground is the church of Vera Cruz. In the background is the city wall and Canonjías quarter, the cathedral cut out against the blue of the sky.

THE FIRST CATHEDRAL
OF ST MARY

Although Segovia boasts such exceptional Roman buildings as the aqueduct, it was not until 1088 that it officially entered history. In that year, Alfonso VI repopulated what had been seven villages, walling the upper part and giving them a legal status. Chartered as a city, Segovia needed a bishop, and therefore a cathedral. In 1115, Don Pedro de Agen took charge of the bishopric. Shortly afterwards, the council gave the chapter the land, which, limited by the city wall, stretches from St Andrew's Church to the *Alcázar*. Here the cathedral and cloister were to be built, along with a residential quarter - the *Claustra* or *Canonjías* - thankfully preserved, complete with hospital and other services. The quarter, cut off from the rest of the city by three gates, had the right of sanctuary and, as it was next to the *Alcázar*, the royal residence, it saw its share of trouble. The War of the *Comuneros* was to put an end to its cloistering and isolation.

The cathedral was between the canons' houses and the fortress, on a landscaped esplanade. It was in the Romanesque style, and must have been somewhat small, but strong and robust, perhaps similar to Zamora cathedral, with which it had much in common concerning position and building dates, and in that it had a mighty bell tower at the west end and was near an *alcázar*. It was vaulted, a unique feature in the Segovian Romanesque, and had a nave with two aisles and a transept. The central apse was dedicated to the Blessed Virgin, the one on the Epistle[*] side to St James and later to St Frutos, and the one on the Gospel[*] side to the Saints John. There was also a crypt dedicated to the Saviour.

Work is known to have been in progress by 1117 and by 1144 it must have been practically finished. It was consecrated on the 16th July 1228, but twenty years later new work was begun on such a scale that it had to be consecrated again in 1257.

Throughout the 15th and 16th Centuries it underwent extensive alterations, of which those carried out on the cloister and east end are of interest to us. The bad condition of the cloister decided Bishop Juan Arias Dávila to have it rebuilt, the famous architect Juan Guas being commissioned to do the work in 1471. Also, in 1509, Juan Gil de Hontañón replaced the Romanesque apse dedicated to St James with a new Gothic one dedicated to St Frutos.

Facing page:

Top: *The cathedral from Fuencisla Heights. In the foreground is the* Alcázar, *the symbol of royal power, and crowning the city is the cathedral. In the background are the Guadarrama Mountains.*

Bottom: *The cathedral from the Ávila road. It is perhaps one of the most suggestive images of the cathedral, and the one described by Ortega y Gasset.*

9

* The Gospel and Epistle sides are, respectively, north and south.

THE NEW CATHEDRAL

In 1521, on the fields of Villalar, an end was brought to the six months of fighting and siege undergone by the cathedral, taken by the *Comuneros** to be better placed to attack the royalists castled up in the *Alcázar*. Although the chronicles tell us of walls pulled down, of tombs opened and screens torn away in the heat of the fray, it certainly could have been rebuilt, as is confirmed by Wyngaerde's drawing of 1562. What, then, brought about the idea of building a new cathedral?

For a long time, the monarchs had always been made to feel uncomfortable by the close presence of such a solid building, which made their fortress less secure, while the canons found their prayers disturbed by the noise of the soldiers and the constant traffic generated by the fortress. Henry IV and Ferdinand the Catholic had already tried to sort things out. Charles V did no more than take advantage of the situation afforded by the war, in which the cathedral had indeed demonstrated its efficacy in the offensive, to remove it from that place. In 1523, Francisco de los Cobos, secretary to the Emperor, wrote to Bishop Pedro de Ribera and to the City Council announcing to them the imperial will: *we have agreed that the cathedral church of your bishopric shall be removed from the place where it now stands to another part of the said city.* The chapter did not receive the news with displeasure, among other reasons, we imagine, because apart from the noise and the disturbances caused by the barracks, the size, lavishness and beauty of the old cathedral did not strike them as adequate. Let us not forget that this was the beginning of the 16th Century, and that Segovia, which had played its part in the introduction of the Renaissance in Castile, was undergoing economic expansion.

Dome of the crossing.
Finished by Francisco Viadero in 1685. The
cross crowning it was put in place this century.

THE FIRST STAGE OF BUILDING, 1525-1557

A site and architects had to be chosen. Thirty years beforehand the Jews had been expelled and the chapter thought, understandably enough, as it owned many of the buildings in the old Jewish quarter, that this was the right area. Furthermore, it was in the city centre and almost at its highest point. As for the architect, there was nobody better than Juan Gil de Hontañón, whom they already knew for he had worked for them in 1509, and he was the famed master of the cathedral of Salamanca.

Facing page: *The cathedral from* El Pinarillo *("The Pine Spinney"). The Clamores valley, the city wall and the buildings serve as a setting to the cathedral , which completes the profile of the medieval city.*

11

* The instigators of an uprising (1520-22) against the policies of King Charles I of Spain, who was also Charles V of Germany and Holy Roman Emperor -*translator's note.*

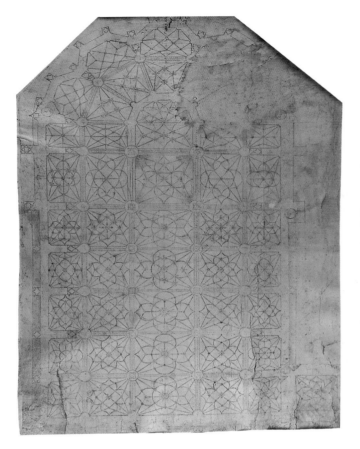

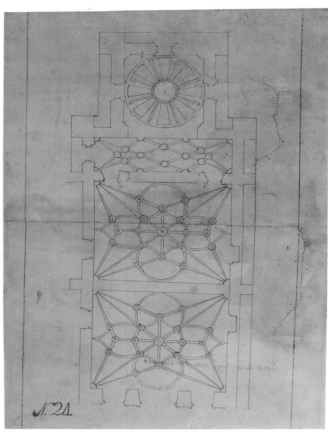

Groundplans
On the left, a groundplan drawn on parchment,
perhaps by Rodrigo Gil de Hontañón, from the
beginning of the 16th Century. On the right, a
plan of the old sacristy, drawn on paper by
Rodrigo Gil de Hontañón in the mid 16th
Century.

In May 1524 the contract was signed. The architectural technician was to be García de Cubillas, upon whose shoulders would fall the burden of steering the works along the right path, when, on the death of Juan and in the absence of his son Rodrigo, they were left without a master. The *fabriquero* (treasurer) chosen, that is, the person in charge of all aspects of administration, was Canon Juan Rodríguez, in some measure the *alma mater* of the undertaking.

Once Juan Gil had drawn the plans and cleared part of the site, on the 24th May 1525, Bishop Diego de Ribera, at the head of a procession and accompanied by many citizens, went to the place where the west face was to be erected. After praying, he took a hoe and struck the ground three times. Thereupon the people began to dig the foundation trenches, which, according to Colmenares, were ready in two weeks. From then on, the cathedral was to be the magnum opus embodying the faith of a people, somewhat repentant after destroying the old see, but above all proud of a church that was to be their symbol.

Fortunately, the cathedral archives keep a set of plans and drawings which, together with many other documents, allow us to retrace the building process step by step. To Juan Gil we could perhaps attribute a plan drawn on parchment showing the design for a church with a nave and two aisles, with side chapels, and the east end with an ambulatory with five pentagonal chapels radiating from it and two square ones at the ends. The whole plan may be inscribed in a double square.

Juan Gil died in April 1526. He was therefore in charge of the works for only ten months, and if we discount the winter months, when work was suspended, he can only have dug the foundation trenches and stockpiled materials. In September, the reins were taken up by his son Rodrigo Gil de Hontañón.

Rodrigo Gil was one of the great figures of Spanish 16th-Century architecture, who left his mark all over Spain and who was able to use simultaneously the Gothic and Renaissance styles. The second plan, also on parchment, perhaps reflects this man's criteria. In general, it follows the first one, but is more harmonious and coherent. No dithering is to be detected in the solving of certain problems, for example the chancel, and above all, and for the first time, certain elements are marked out.

Rodrigo remained as master of the works until July 1529, when he was dismissed, the reason not being known. If we follow the account written years later by Juan Rodríguez, then work began at the west face and perimeter walls, where it went on simultaneously. If to this we add the fact that the cloister was finished by July 1529, we may deduce how much was done by the time Rodrigo left.

In 1524, even before the new church was begun, an agreement had been made with the architectural technician Juan Campero to dismantle the cloister built by Juan Guas in 1471 and move it to the new site. This, a real technical feat for its time, as seen by contemporaries and those who came later, may have been due to reasons of economy, but certain details such as the increased height or the removal and rebuilding of all of the tracery and finally the doorway lead us to think that æsthetic intentions were also involved. Be that as it may, the rebuilding work was over by July 1529. We may conclude from this that, as it forms part of the south face of the cathedral, around that time the vaulting of the side chapels was about to be made, it being on record that St Catherine's Chapel, the bottom storey of the tower, was vaulted in 1530.

With Rodrigo's departure, the burden passed onto the shoulders of García de Cubillas, the architectural technician who was aided by the prudence and good advice of Juan Rodríguez. From 1529 to 1542, when the nave was closed and the first stage of the building was concluded, responsibility was shared between them and so, despite sporadic visits by Rodrigo in 1532-33, we must consider them as the real masters. García de Cubillas was in fact appointed to the post, in recognition of his merits and his work, in 1536.

The building was at a critical point in 1530. If, on the face of it, the vaulting of the chapels offered no special difficulty, the nave and aisles were a different matter. This was how the chapter saw it, and they did not hesitate to call in the experts of the day: Juan de Alava, Bigarny, Egas and Francisco de Colonia.

A report has been preserved drawn up by Enrique Egas, the master of Toledo Cathedral, dated 3rd March 1532. From it we know that eight of the ten inter-buttress chapels had been roofed over, that the west face had been erected up to their level and that twenty metres of the tower had been built. He judged everything thus far done to be good and advised that Rodrigo Gil's plans should be followed. He then went on to considerations of a technical nature - the width and quality of the pillars - and æsthetic ones, but what he was most preoccupied with was the business of proportions. In his opinion, the model to be followed was the height of the chapels, that is fifty feet. On this basis, the aisles would need a height of 75 feet and the nave 115. If this recommendation were followed, then the church would be very beautiful. He was not in favour of slenderness, or of the aisles being of the same height as the nave, as this would make the building darker inside. Finally, and at the behest of Juan Rodríguez, he suggested a wall should be built at the crossing so that the nave and aisles could be used while the east end was being built.

Francisco de Colonia's report is dated 1536, by which year the pillars had reached the same height as the capitals of the chapels, the buttresses were in place, as were the windows of the aisles, the west face was higher than the chantries inside and the bell tower was on the point of surpassing twenty metres. He advised vaulting the aisles in order to counterbalance the nave.

Ambulatory.
Stone commemorating the consecration of the church, which took place in 1768. The cathedral is dedicated to the Assumption and to St Frutos.

From the date of the report to 1538, the flying buttresses and strainer arches were erected and by 1539, the stretch of the nave and aisles adjacent to the crossing was closed in. From this it would seem that Colonia's advice was not followed and that the nave and aisles were vaulted simultaneously.

Once the covering of this part had been experimented on, work went on speedily and by the end of 1541, the main body of the church had been finished off, the design of the ribbing being respected but not the decoration of the bosses, as we shall see. With great satisfaction, Juan Rodríguez wrote: *And so on the said day* [2nd January 1542] *I gave Juan Pérez the contractor* [33 maravedís] *to offer a lunch to the tradesmen and labourers to celebrate the closing of the whole nave of the church achieved on the eve of the last birthday of Our Lord Jesus Christ.*

The Bell Tower

After the building of the wall between the nave and aisles and the space reserved for the future crossing, and the glazing of the windows from 1544 to 1549, this part of the building came into use. Meanwhile, all efforts went into the building of the magnificent bell tower. About 1550, work was under way on the belfry and two years later on the square terrace on which was to sit the octagonal stone structure with four corner buttresses, which was to support the wooden spire covered in sheets of lead and topped out in 1558. This little finishing touch was destroyed by fire in 1614 and replaced with the present dome, designed by Pedro de Brizuela.

The Chapter-House

Around the same period, whilst awaiting the start of the east end, the builders put up other departments necessary for the chapter to be able to go about its business. So, in 1544, work began on the chapter-house and library, the block given over to it being built onto the southern face of the tower. In 1555, it was considered finished. Jerome of Antwerp participated in the sculpture work.

THE SECOND STAGE OF THE BUILDING, 1560-77

In the twenty years ensuing after the finishing of the nave and aisles and before the recommencement of the work and the drawing of the plans of the east end - 1560 - the chapter-house, belfry and other minor works were completed, all of them necessary for the inauguration of that part, which took place in solemnity on the 15th August 1558, the day of the Assumption of Our Lady, to which the cathedral is consecrated.

The nave and aisles were used for Divine service, but the need was felt for a fitting presbytery in line with the part in use, as was, more especially, the need to finish off the church that was the pride of Segovia. In 1559 García de Cubillas must have died. Lacking a master of works, the chapter decided to turn to Rodrigo Gil, at the time in Salamanca, for nobody would be as capable as he of carrying on and taking up the challenge of planning the east end. In November 1560 the contract was drawn up. Until his death, in 1574, he lived in Segovia and was buried in its cathedral. However, the activity set in motion by this architect, apart from the demolition of the Convent of St Clare, in order to clear the site, was centred on the sacristy, finished in 1572, on the doorway of which he was carried away by Renaissance ideas.

Chevet.
Rodrigo Gil was right to choose the traditional polygonal shape for the east end.

Facing page:
The bulk of the cathedral overshadows the buildings once inhabited by the Jewish community. The impact of its volume has attracted the attention of painters and writers, among them Gómez de la Serna, who felt strongly attracted by the mighty tower.

The cathedral at the end of Real Street *("Royal Street", or "High Street"), Segovia's busiest thoroughfare. In the foreground is St Martin's churchyard.*

Without a doubt the most difficult part of our building's history to chronicle is that of the east end, as many of the documents concerning the last years of the 16th Century are missing, although it is possible to retrace the general development of the building process. In 1561, the foundations were laid for the front two pillars of the crossing and in 1563 the first stone went into place of the polygonal wall of the apse, in front of which Gil designed a square presbytery, with the same area as the crossing, rather than the rectangular one drawn on the plan, which, under the terms of the contract, he was committed to maintaining. In this change, and in the choice of a polygonal chevet rather than a straight one, we must infer the influence of Juan Rodríguez, who, with so many years' experience, was by then an expert.

By the time of Juan Gil's death, the whole length of the ambulatory and its chapels had been laid out and built up to the height of the corbels of the vault springers, the Ionic capitals of which were, as it were, the master's signature.

THE THIRD STAGE OF BUILDING: THE BAROQUE MASTERS, 1577-1684

It was by now impossible for coming masters to alter the Gothic form of the church by offering the excuse of the æsthetic considerations of the Baroque style. On the other hand, the building of San Lorenzo de El Escorial, near Segovia, took up the best architects and workers of Castile. Indeed, no man of the stature of Rodrigo was available until the appointment in 1607 of Pedro de Brizuela. These were difficult times: Segovia's economy was not so healthy, which, coupled with a series of personal misfortunes, was to drag the work out and out. In short, however, the process went on like this: 1590 saw the building of the arch of the chapel giving onto that of the Holy Sacrament - the Sacristy - (the first one on the right of the ambulatory) which was to serve as a model for the rest, to which Bartolomé de Lorriaga and Bartolomé de la Pedraja committed themselves in 1591. In 1601 conditions were signed for the completion of the ambulatory according to plans by Rodrigo del Solar, little of which, if anything, would by carried out. In 1651, the chancel was still without a vault and was covered with temporary roofing. A year later work was going on on the south arm of the transept and it was not until 1671, the date painted on the wall of the apse, that the ambulatory was finished. The refinement of the Gothic and Renaissance mouldings gave rise to a greater clumsiness of style, very noticeable in the Tuscan capitals of the springers, which are not well made.

There was still a part open to the sky, one offering serious technical problems, the crossing. Juan Rodríguez, who had learnt the lesson of the collapse of the tambours of Seville and Burgos had insisted that the four pillars of the crossing holding up Segovia's dome should be quite substantial. Rodrigo Gil had not planned a Gothic tambour but a Renaissance dome, which would be taken up again, albeit with alterations to bring it into line with the fashion of the day, by the Segovian Pedro de Brizuela in 1630. In 1632, owing to the architect's death, work was halted. From 1649 on, different names and opinions followed one after another. In 1660, Francisco del Campo Agüero presented his plan to the chapter. In the end, it was Francisco Viadero who had the honour of finishing off the dome, and with it the cathedral, in 1685. On the 8th June 1686, the wall that had separated the nave and aisles from the east end for fifty years was pulled down. The people of Segovia then broke out *in cries of joy and thanksgiving*. The consecration ceremony was postponed until the 16th July 1768.

The Outside

The whole of the cathedral, and its relationship with the city, can only be taken in from some distance, but it is worth the effort to go over to the *Hoyos* ("Holes")* or *Pinarillo* ("Pine Spinney") road, to the Fuencisla or Parral Heights and to the beginning of the Ávila road, as from any of these places the sight is incomparable and justifies so many writings and paintings. From close by, the cathedral gradually opens up to a more painstaking and subtle perception.

We can begin our walk round it on the south side, stretching along Barrionuevo, San Geroteo and Refitolería Streets. From the slope of Barrionuevo

*So-called for crossing the site of an ancient cemetery - *translator's note*.

The chevet of the cathedral
The position of the cathedral on the west side of the Main Square prevented the square from being laid out properly according to the plans made by the Segovian architect Pedro de Brizuela in the 17th Century.

17

Doorways of the cathedral. On the left, the Main, or Pardon Doorway. The mullion bears an image of Our Lady. On the right, the north (St Frutos's) end of the transept.

(Lit. *New Quarter*) Street, which was given this name once the Jews had been turned out of the district, it appears as a cascade of pinnacles detained by a flat gable end. Such an austere façade, very much in line with the Castilian Baroque, was planned by Francisco Viadero for offices around 1671, during the episcopate of Don Martín Moratinos, whose shield emblazons the central balcony. Along the whole length of the cornice a row of pinnacles and the openwork balustrade link it with the Gothic cresting behind it.

Continuing our walk along San Geroteo Street, named after the legendary first bishop of the diocese, between the Chapel of the Tabernacle and the Cloister, we come to the south end of the transept, very sober and with a long history, as it was not to be finished until Pedro de Brizuela completed it in the 17th Century. The mullion is adorned with an 18th-Century statue of the bishop-saint.

The rhythm of the buttresses on the blind wall of the cloister takes us to the junction of Doctor Castelo and Almuzara Streets. In few places is it possible to form such an accurate idea of how important volume and walls are in Spanish architecture. The vast mass of the tower, made more so by the lower ground, rises clean and solemn, ignorant of Gothic transparency and grace. Pedro de Brizuela's dome, built in 1620, accentuates its bulk.

A downhill walk past a sloping wall, adorned with pyramids and lions holding the arms of Spain, the City and the Chapter in their claws, leads our steps to Marqués del Arco Street, popularly known as Lion Street, for the sculptures. Before us is the west face and in front of it a lonely graveyard bordered by the wall and carpeted with the tombstones that until the end of the 18th Century covered the floors of the nave and aisles. This square, known as the *Enlosado* ("Flagged Place"), always closed off and with access from the inside came into

being as a result of the wishes of the chapter and the city council. So beautiful did the cathedral seem to them that, so that nothing should obscure it, they forbade anything to be built onto it and even decided to clear the surroundings. So, at the end of the 16th Century, houses were demolished *to embellish the front*. Some time into the Baroque period, the area was enclosed within the wall with the pyramids and lions. The granite steps were rebuilt by J. Odriozola in 1899, when gates were made to protect the place.

We now come round to the west face, where no concession is made to decoration save the Blessed Virgin on the mullion of the Doorway of Pardon, and the arches over it. The buttresses and the cornices show what the inside is going to be like. On the right-hand side is the bell tower, and further away, in line with it, the chapter-house and library. On the left is the Almuzara turret.

The Almuzara turret, which takes its name from the old name of the street in which it stands (*Almuzara* is the Arabic word for a military exercise area), one of the busiest in the city, is really a spiral staircase with a dome designed in 1626 by Brizuela to match the one on the bell tower. In the lower part a beautiful shield of Spain from Charles V's time is to be admired.

Going towards the Main Square (*Plaza Mayor*), we may see the north face, with the stepped heights of the nave and aisles and, between the buttresses bearing the shields of Segovia (the aqueduct), the Chapter (a vase) and Bishop Diego de Ribera, some lower buildings, like sacristies, added by Pedro de Brizuela in 1621.

At the north end of the transept is St Frutos's Door, practically the only one in use. Its history fated, it was finished in the time of Pedro de Brizuela, who had designed it. Despite the more or less justified criticism it has come in for - it is

Left, *St Frutos's Doorway, by Pedro de Brizuela, completed in 1633. In the niche is the statue of the saint.*

Right, *St Geroteo's Doorway, in the south arm of the transept, completed well into the Baroque period but in the style of the main doorway.*

obvious that neither the granite nor the style harmonize with the rest of the building - it is an interesting piece. It was planned in 1608 but not finished until 1633. Such a long period of building may be explained by the economic crisis of the day. In fact, the design of the doorway is a scaled-down version of the one at San Lorenzo de El Escorial. In two storeys, the upper one repeats the motif on a smaller scale. In the niche is the statue of St Frutos, patron saint of Segovia, sculpted in 1611 by Felipe de Aragón. There was some debate as to whether to use the side niches for St Peter and St Paul or St Valentine and St Engracia, and when it was decided to house the latter two in them, the decision came to no effect. As for the shields of the chapter and the city adorning the squinches that join the façade with the aisles, they were made by Brizuela in 1612.

In 1804 the decision was taken to protect the cathedral from rubbish and other troublesome matters so work began on the raised platform that starts in "Lion Street" and continues, on pedestals, along the line of balls according to plans drawn by Juan de la Torre y López, although, when he fell ill, it may have been finished by Antonio Pérez. At the end of the 19th Century the gates were fitted. In the space marked off by the pillars once stood the unfinished Chapel of St Frutos, designed by Giambattista Sachetti, and the *Haceduría* (cathedral offices), planned as such and as a balcony for watching the bulls from by Pedro de Brizuela, Pedro Monasterio, Mugaguren and others in 1613, and demolished in 1800 at the suggestion of the Royal Academy of Fine Arts of St Ferdinand, who wished the chevet to be exposed.

Finally, on the round wall of the tower there are two shields. The first is of the cathedral chapter, and the second, dated 1571, is of Philip II, crowned by a curious emblem: two joined hands with a flame and the motto *Ignis Amoris*.

The Inside

The crossing is the ideal place from which to take in the grandeur and luminosity of this cathedral.

The Nave and Aisles

Although the outside retains a purity of style and offers a roundness of volumes, it may be somewhat guilty of sobriety. The interior, on the other hand, is the epitome of elegance, thanks to the care taken in its proportions, the refinement of its mouldings, and light. Looking towards the west, even allowing for the choir screen, the sequence of the nave, aisles and side chapels is of great beauty. This part, let us not forget that it was built between 1525 and 1542, keeps a perfect oneness of form. Though of different styles, the vaults of the chapels match each other in pairs on either side. In the three halls, the repetition of one model was preferred, much after the taste of the Hontañóns, the only difference being that the bosses in the stretch next to the crossing bear the monogram I.H.S., while on the rest, Jerome of Antwerp (?) put scenes concerning the Blessed Virgin and Christ (with Adam and Eve in the third sections of the aisles), with other subjects on the secondary bosses, sometimes related to those on the main ones, which do not appear to keep to any narrative sequence amongst themselves. Their height (thirty-three metres) does not allow them to be examined with the naked eye.

The pillars carry a delicate and complex moulding, becoming a mere abstraction on the bases, much in fashion at the end of the Gothic period. Their journey up to the vault ribs is broken only on the main shafts, by small capitals, whose size makes them look higher than they really are.

Facing page: *Nave.*
The choir, crossing and chancel, with Sabatini's reredos.

Following double page:

Left: *Crossing.*
The story of the closing of the crossing is long and includes several plans, from the Gothic and Renaissance ones to the final one by Pedro de Brizuela (1630) completed by Francisco Viadero in 1685.

Right: *Ambulatory.*
Together with the dome of the crossing, this was the last part of the cathedral to be built, although it respected the original plans, which explains why only a careful examination will discover the mark of the 17th Century in the profiles and bosses of the ribs.

*Nave and aisles.
From the west end of the church we may clearly
see the retrochoir, planned at the end of the 18th
Century by Juan de Villanueva and Ventura
Rodríguez.*

To the conceptual clarity and the eurhythmy, we must add light. Although originally mullions and tracery had been planned, these elements were only ever included in the windows of the chapels, never in the higher lights. In this way, more light was let in and the stained-glass windows were enhanced in size and legibility. If we bear in mind also the fact that during the 17th century, an absolutely imperceptible coat of whitewash was applied, among other reasons, to even out the colour of the ashlars, few are the buildings we can admire with so much light. The cathedral's luminosity, however, is not that of colour and symbolic of the Gothic period, but that of the pure light of the Renaissance and Baroque.

There are other details of interest. It is known that Segovia Cathedral is Salamanca's younger sister, and that it brings a close to the Gothic chapter in Spain. Its construction, what happened in other cathedrals and the experience gathered down the centuries are reflected not only in the conception of space but also in technical problems like the solution of the gangway in the nave or the four pillars of the crossing, of ashlars throughout their diameter.

Transept

The transept was finished at the end of the 17th Century, and the discerning eye may detect one or two unpolished details, for example the odd Classicist capitals. Over the crossing, Brizuela's dome, the heir to Rodrigo Gil's original idea, is supported by pendentives decorated with reliefs of the four evangelists, clumsily sculpted by Andrés Monasterio.

The East End

Rodrigo Gil conceived this part, following the good advice of Juan Rodríguez, in absolute concord with the previous one, so much so that the capitals with Ionic imposts in the apsidal chapels in no way clash with the ribs springing from them. The complex vault over the chancel is late 17th Century.

Rodrigo Gil was so subtle and refined that hardly anyone notices that in the ambulatory, that is the continuation of the naves, he used the same elevation as in the nave - arcading, walkways and windows - rather than the one that might reasonably have been expected. He was not, however, so subtle with the design of the windows in the first section, as these are clumsily made and ugly, partly because of the limited space where they had to be installed.

To Rodrigo Gil we also owe the entrance door to the old sacristy, today the Chapel of the Holy Sacrament, which is completely Renaissance. It is made up of a central arch and two lintelled doorways, the whole abounding in elements typical of Hontañón. Over the lintels are the arms of the chapter and in the central niche is a small Baroque reredos.

Floor

Until the end of the 18th Century, the nave and aisles were used as a cemetery, their floor made up of the canons' granite tombstones. In 1787, shortly before work was begun on the retrochoir, the decision was made to lay a floor of red, white and blue stone following a design by Juan de la Torre y López.

The care with which the work was carried out is attested to by the minute piece next to St Peter's Chapel. Every cathedral has its magic spot, and this one's is here. I remember seeing, as a boy, elderly people, in a strange symbiosis of religion and superstition, kissing the piece to save the building. Passing the hand over it will reveal the concavity that such a curious custom was to bring about.

*Facing page:
Epistle Nave.
Building lasted from 1525 to 1541. Artistic
decoration is limited to the bosses and vaults,
enhancing the sensation of height and elegance.
The photograph on the left shows the nave
looking towards the ambulatory and the one on
the right, looking towards the west face.*

THE STAINED-GLASS WINDOWS

Stained-glass windows are a worthy complement for any cathedral. They shelter it from the outside, they let light in and are, at the same time, polished examples of art, where colour reaches its uttermost expression and the faithful may read, as if told in a comic, the great story of the Redemption of man.

Soon after the vaulting of the nave and aisles was completed, Juan Rodríguez was commissioned to travel to Burgos and other churches in order to gather information about stained glass. On his return, he wrote a report in which he set out the subjects to be illustrated and the order they should follow in Segovia, which was kept to almost literally. Glaziers capable of carrying out the work were then chosen and work commenced. They were Pierre of Hollad, Pierre de Chiberri, Walter of Ronch, Nicolás de Holanda and Nicolás de Vergara. The Pierres worked on site, Walter of Ronch in Antwerp, Nicolás de Holanda in Salamanca and Nicolás de Vergara in Toledo. The installation of the windows was begun in 1544 and finished in 1549. Around that time the medieval system of narrative had given way to the great compositions, easier to read, as we may appreciate here. In short, they are a good example of Mannerist æsthetics, which also lets more light in.

The curious visitor may follow the three cycles developed throughout the building. The first one, the Mystery of the Redemption, in the nave and aisles; the second one, the Life of the Blessed Virgin, in the transept; and the third, Jesus's public life, in the ambulatory. As for the windows of the chancel, which are 20th Century, and which do not form a story, we shall examine them when we come to the chancel.

Let us begin, then, with the first cycle, many of the windows of which on the south side are so deformed that the scenes are barely recognizable. Juan Rodríguez himself said that the series would begin with the Angel's Greeting and end with the Ascension, *from the first window of the side chapels (sections) to the epistle side following the order of reading, for this is the purpose of the pictures for those who do not know.*

Each window is in three parts, the middle one has a New Testament subject, concerning Christ's Life and Passion, accompanied on the sides by closely related episodes from the Old Testament, according to the well-known formula. To facilitate identification, the book and chapter they are taken from are given in cartouches. Some also bear the date.

We should then begin our walk in the section of the epistle (north) aisle adjacent to the crossing and follow along the gospel (south) aisle, to continue down

Preceding double page:

Left: *Nave.*
Vaults over the choir, finished between 1539 and 1541.

Right: *Chancel.*
The Gothic vaults with their complicated ribbing are 17th Century.

Facing page: *Nave and south aisle. The stained-glass windows in the nave, aisles and chancel allow us to appreciate the stepping in their arrangement.*

Stained glass.
The first section of the south side of the nave. It is
by Walter of Ronch.
On the left, Esther and Ahasuerus.
In the centre, the Prayers in the Garden, with
what may be the Alcázar.
On the right, the prophet Daniel.
It is dated 1545.

the nave. We shall just point out the subjects, without going into their meaning, which would take up many pages.

South aisle: *First window* (over the Chapel of the Christ of Solace or of the entrance to the cloister) Annunciation of the Birth of Isaac - Annunciation - Annunciation of the birth of Samson (Nicolás de Vergara, 1544). *Second:* Judith triumphant - The visit to St Elizabeth - the return of Tobias (Nicolás de Holanda, 1544). *Third:* Aaron's rod - The Nativity - Moses and the burning bush (Walter of Ronch, 1544). *Fourth:* Circumcision of Abraham - The Circumcision - Circumcision of Joshua (Pierres, 1548). *Fifth:* Solomon and the Queen of Sheba - The Adoration of the Magi - the fleet of Hiram, King of Tyre (Pierres, 1548).

West face. *First:* The Purification (Pierres, 1545). *Second:* The Flight to Egypt (Pierres, 1545).

North aisle: *First*, over the Chapel of the Conception: Pharaoh in the Red Sea - The Baptism - Moses and the Waters of Meribah (Pierres, 1545). *Second:* The trials of Job - The Temptation - Joshua accused by the Devil (Nicolás de Holanda, 1544). *Third:* The Shunammite woman at the feet of Elisha - Mary Magdalen washing Christ's feet - Elijah raising the son of the widow of Zarephath (Nicolás de Vergara, 1546). *Fourth:* The Passover - Christ's Entry into Jerusalem - David

Stained glass.
The first section of the north side of the nave,
after the west end. It is by the Pierres and dated
1547. On the left, Moses and the bronze serpent.
In the centre, the Crucifixion and on the right the
institution of the Passover.

with Solomon riding a mule (Walter of Ronch, 1545). *Fifth:* Melchizedek and Abraham - The Last Supper - The Manna (Pierres, 1545).

Nave, south side. *First:* Esther and Ahasuerus - the Prayers in the Garden - the Prophet Daniel (Walter of Ronch, 1545). *Second:* Joseph sold by his brothers - the Arrest - Queen Jezebel (Pierres, 1546, badly damaged). *Third:* Jeremiah scourged - The Scourging - Isaiah (Walter of Ronch, 1545, very badly damaged). *Fourth:* Cyrus and Daniel - Christ before Pilate - the Blinding of Samson (Pierres, 1546, unrecognizable). *Fifth:* Isaac - Christ bearing His Cross - Naomi returning to Bethlehem (Pierres, 1546, badly damaged).

Nave, north side. *First:* Moses and the bronze serpent - The Crucifixion - Institution of the Passover (Pierres, 1547). *Second:* Samson before Gaza - the Taking Down - Jonah and the whale (Pierres, 1547). *Third:* David and the Amalekites - the Descent into Limbo - the Israelites leaving Egypt (Pierres, 1548). *Fourth:* Samson leaving Gaza - The Resurrection - Jonah coming out of the whale (Pierres, 1548). *Fifth:* the Story of Enoch (Pierres, 1548) - Ascension - Elijah taken up to Heaven.

West face. Top window. It once showed the Final Judgement, replaced at the end of the 18th Century with plain panes.

31

Stained-glass window over the Chapel of the Conception. The Crossing of the Red Sea, which subject anticipates the Baptism of Christ. Pierres (1545).

Stained glass.
First section of the south aisle.
The Baptism of Christ.
The work of the Pierres, dated 1544.

The second cycle concerns the Life of the Blessed Virgin, is to be found in the crossing and begins with the window in the southeast corner, ending with the adjacent one in the ambulatory. *First:* Nativity of the Blessed Virgin. *Second* (south rose): Angel musicians. *Third:* Presentation in the Temple. *Fourth:* Betrothal of the Virgin. *Fifth:* Pentecost. *Sixth:* Death of the Virgin. *Seventh* (north rose): Angel musicians. *Eighth:* Assumption. *Ninth:* Coronation. *Tenth:* The Immaculate Conception.

Stained-glass window.
It was made by Nicolás de Holanda in 1544 and
depicts the tempting of Job and Joshua accused
by the Devil, Old Testament themes in line with
the Tempting of Christ in the central pane.

Although the cycle about the Blessed Virgin had been proposed by Juan Rodríguez, it is known that the windows were not put in place until the 17th Century, once the crossing had been closed, which explains the presence of the Immaculate Conception.

These windows, like those of the east end, were made by Francisco Herranz, verger of the cathedral from 1674 to 1689 and are very interesting for the world of glass inasmuch as Francisco Herranz and Juan Danis rediscovered the technique of colour, long since forgotten. The archives preserve documents written by each of them: Danis's *Tratado de la fábrica de vidrio* ("Treatise on the Making of Glass") and Herranz's *Modo con que Francisco Herranz...executó las cincuenta y quatro vidrieras...*("The means whereby Francisco Herranz...wrought the fifty-four windows").

Let us see then the series closing the east end. *In the month of April 1774 the removal began of the stained-glass windows in the Chancel, which showed the Apostles, and the two largest ones the imprisonment and martyrdom of St Peter and the six in the aisles different episodes from the life of Christ...*Indeed, as we shall see, they were replaced with plain glass windows in order to let more light onto Sabatini's reredos, cutting short the iconographic programme. We shall therefore describe those remaining in the ambulatory, beginning on the left. All of them are about the Public Life of Christ and deal mainly with His miracles.

Windows of the ambulatory. *First:* Visit of Nicodemus - Casting out the Merchants from the Temple - Casting out the devil from the dumb man. *Second:* The healing of St Peter's mother-in-law - the Samaritan woman - the woman afflicted by hæmorrhages. *Third:* the Healing of the deaf-mute - the Healing at the Pool of Bethesda - the Healing of the man with dropsy. *Fourth:* The Calling of Peter and Andrew - Peter's Mission - The Calming of the Storm (let us not forget that this window is on the axis of the church and those in the Chancel also refer to the first apostle). *Fifth:* St Peter taking a didrachm from the fish's mouth - the Feeding of the Five Thousand - Cursing of the fig tree. *Sixth:* the Raising of the son of the widow of Nain - the adulteress - Healing of the daughter of the Canaanite woman. *Seventh:* Healing of the man with the withered hand - Healing of the man who had been blind since birth - Healing of the man with palsy.

THE CHAPELS

Now that the history of the building of the cathedral has been told, we must guide the visitor around the various chapels and other parts of the building, but in this church bereft of any decoration, he will not find - with few exceptions - those masterpieces of art that are the pride of other churches. Most of the religious objects and furniture of the old cathedral of St Mary disappeared with its destruction, and when the new see was almost ready, the coffers were drained and the city was going into a long economic decline. The cathedral is, in itself, the most beautiful piece, and the pleasure of beholding it is enough.

As in any cathedral, space was defined and limited according to its use: there is a place for the chapter, one for the people and another for private worship. It would seem appropriate to begin with the most important one and then continue round without retracing our steps, as we assume that the visitor will come in through St Frutos's Door and leave the same way.

CHOIR AND CHANCEL

The cathedral is the bishop's see and the church of the chapter, and for them the noblest part is marked off and reserved: the Chancel and the choir, situated in the centre of the building and joined by the *valla* ("fence") or sacred way.

The choir occupies the third and fourth sections. Its upper and lower stalls have a total of one hundred and sixteen places, including the two reserved for the king and queen, and the bishop's throne, the former at either end of the upper stalls and the latter at the back and presiding over the rest. The stalls are in the Gothic style, with a geometric pattern on the backs, based on the rectangle and circle in the lower row, and on windows with mullions and tracery in the upper one. Only on the arms, and then contained in little circles, do we find naturalist subjects, most of them grotesque, as was the fashion of the time, unlike the misericords, which are severely sober. The upper stalls are decorated with canopies, atop fine columns, forming a continuous front decorated throughout with ogee arches and tracery, with the exception of the stall next to the king's, which, despite its simpler design, may originally have been the one reserved for the bishop - the nearest one to the altar - relegated when the royal stalls were carved and the bishop's place was put in its present position. It was then that it was given its greater size and the back was adorned with the arms of Bishop Arias Dávila, whose episcopate lasted from 1461 to 1497. The canopy over it was remade by Huici in 1789.

The royal choirstalls are more interesting. The one at the southern end has four shields of Castile and Portugal, for Queen Joan, the wife of Henry IV, and the one at the northern end has another four shields of Castile, all of them polychromed. Over them are pointed canopies crowned respectively by a herald holding the shield of Castile and a standard-bearing lion vanquishing a Saracen, that is to say the king who was defender of the faith. By tradition, Henry IV liked to attend

Facing page: *The organ in the south aisle was built by the organ-makers Pedro and José de Chavarria in 1770. The beautiful console enclosing it follows the design of the cabinet maker Juan Maurat, the maker of other pieces in the cathedral.*

Following double page:

Left and right:
The organ in the north aisle was made by Pedro Liborna Chavarria in 1702 and is an excellent example of Spanish organ-making. It stands against the 18th-Century retrochoir adorned with the statue of St Matthew, by Manuel Adeba Pacheco.

Middle: *Drawing of the console of the organ in the south aisle. It is preserved in the archives and the one in the gospel aisle was also based on it.*

The Choir.
On the left, the lectern, attributed to atelier of
Vasco de la Zarza, in whose circle the first local
manifestations of the Renaissance were noticed.
On the right, the back of King Henry IV's seat,
with the arms of Castile and León and
pomegranates, the King's emblem: "It is
bittersweet to reign".

Facing page:
The choirstalls are 15th Century and were
brought from the old cathedral. When they were
installed in the new one, more stalls were added
and some alterations were made, such as the
handrails.

Divine worship in the choir, whence the importance and pre-eminence given to these seats.

The choir came mainly from the old cathedral and was moved here and installed in 1558 by the carvers Juan Gil and Jerome of Antwerp, who added four stalls to each row and the side pieces of the bishop's throne, decorated with Grotesque work. As late as 1789 Fermín Huici, a cabinet maker from La Granja, made ten more choirstalls for each row, necessitated by the enlarging occasioned by work on the retrochoir, respecting the style of the old ones and contributing an early example of the neo-Gothic.

In the centre of the choir is the lectern, on a beautiful Renaissance stand, adorned with trophies and attributed to the 16th-Century carver Vasco de la Zarza.

The area is finished off by two great organs, with golden, festive-looking consoles that completely fill the archways they stand in, reaching right up to the keystones. The one on the epistle side was donated by Bishop Ocampo and was built by the organ-maker Pedro Liborna Chavarria in 1702. The one on the gospel side was a gift from Bishop J. José Martínez Escalzo and was made in 1770 by Pedro and José Chavarria, Pedro's grandsons. We owe the lavish console of this organ to the carver Juan Maurat. These magnificent organs say much of the splendour enjoyed by music, so closely linked with the solemnity of liturgy in the cathedral, where the famous *Cancionero del Alcázar* ("*Alcázar* Song-book") is preserved and which had amongst its masters Correa de Arauxo, who died in one of the houses of the Canonjías district - at number 19 Daoiz Street, to be precise .

The choir is enclosed by a Baroque screen, installed in 1729 and wrought at Elgóibar by Antonio de Elorza, who came from a famous family of screen-makers

Nave.
In the foreground is the Sacred Way, which joins the presbytery with the choir, which is enclosed by the screen forged by Antonio de Elorza and installed in 1729.

and who made most of those to be seen in this cathedral. As we shall have the opportunity to see, the Elorzas' atelier produced most of the Baroque screens protecting the chapels and which, with slight variations, follow a pattern of two tiers separated by friezes, three columns and an intricate topping of leafwork and medallions. The more intricately worked parts of the bars are covered in gold leaf, as are the friezes and finishing pieces, which in no way detracts from the sobriety emanating from them.

The fifth section and the crossing were reserved for the faithful, which meant that for the priests to be able to get from the choir to the presbytery, a passage was necessary, bordered by railings - "the fence" - also by Antonio Elorza, and with the flooring made of the tombstones of several bishops. To the left, and joined to one of the crossing pillars, stands the marble pulpit with the ducal arms of the Albuquerque family and figures of the Immaculate Conception and the four evangelists, which came from the now defunct convent of St Francis at Cuéllar, where the Albuquerques were the local lords, and came to our cathedral as a result of the 19th-Century Disentailment (whereby much Church property was confiscated and sold off -*translator's note*).

The end of the sacred way leads into the Chancel, a space reserved for the chapter and where liturgy is held with solemnity. When this part was finished, as

Pulpit.
It was taken from the disentailed church of St Francis of Cuéllar, of the foundation of the House of Albuquerque, with whose arms it is decorated. It was installed in the cathedral last century.

we have seen, well into the 17th Century, the great naked walls of the apse would never receive the many-scened reredos for which they were doubtlessly designed. We do know of the existence of a silver altar, but no more is known about it except that, considering it unfitting, the chapter replaced it with the present one. In 1767, the members of the chapter asked Charles III for permission to build the reredos, which was given, the piece to be paid for from the property confiscated from the Jesuits. Francisco Sabatini, the king's favourite architect, prepared several plans for the king to chose from.

The altarpiece, which was made in the workshops of the Royal Palace in Madrid, consists of a predella, a central storey with four Corinthian columns, a variation much to the architect's taste, and a heavy upper part bearing Mary's monogram against a glory of clouds and angels. It is dedicated to the Blessed Virgin under the advocation of Our Lady of Peace, who presides from the central niche, and the three traditional Segovian saints and the first bishop, at the express wish of the chapter: St Frutos and St Geroteo, in the intercolumns, and St Valentine and St Engracia (St Frutos's brother and sister), on the upper storey. They are all made of wood covered in white stucco and are by Manuel Adeba Pacheco. The Virgin is an exquisite Gothic piece, perhaps French, which, according to tradition, was donated by Henry IV. The ivory face and hands stand out

Chancel.
Our Lady of Peace, a Gothic image, whose silver
garments were retouched in 1770 by Antonio F.
Vendetti, who also made the throne.

Facing page: *Main reredos.*
This sumptuous marble altarpiece was designed
by Francisco Sabatini and completed in 1775. In
the centre is the Virgin of Peace, and in the
intercolumns are St Frutos and St Geroteo,
respectively the patron saint and first bishop of
the diocese. At the top are St Valentine and St
Engracia. The four statues are by Manuel Adeba.

against the silver clothing, which was retouched in the 1770s by the Roman silversmith Antonio Fabio Vendetti, who also made the throne, the monstrance (now in the cathedral offices) and the six tall candlesticks that used to grace this place and are now on show in St Catherine's Chapel. The six silver candlesticks now here, as well as the sacring tablets, are by the Cordoban goldsmith Damián de Castro and are dated 1769, while the great altar lights are by the silversmith José Pérez and are dated 1739.

This ornate reredos, a showcase of all the marbles available from Spanish quarries, in consonance with the economic feeling of encouraging the use of national resources, was begun in 1770 and finished on the 28th July 1775. It was consecrated on the 7th September and the first mass was held, for which occasion Chapel master Juan Montón y Mallen, composed a mass. The piece was admired in court circles close to Sabatini, who, proud of his work, wanted to set it off by giving it more light, for which reason he took down the stained glasswork from the windows of the chapel and the immediate sections of the nave in 1794 and replaced them with plain glass. A year later he also removed the window in the west face, dedicated to the Last Judgement. Not content with that, he tried to stucco the walls, obviously following the fashion established in the chapels off the

Bottom:
Wooden bust of St Geroteo, by Mateo de Negrete,
in the finishing piece of a screen in the chancel.

ambulatory, but met with the opposition of the chapter, who were thinking of covering them with cloth.

In 1916, owing to the festival of the coronation of Our Lady of Fuencisla, the patron of the city, the space was changed, the marble balustrade being moved forward and the flooring renewed. It was then that new glasswork was installed in the windows of the apse, from the workshops of Maumejean, with the well-known images of the Segovian saints, the Blessed Virgin, St Geroteo, St Remigio - patron saint of the then bishop - and of the Segovian Jesuit St Alonso Rodríguez. Shortly afterwards, around 1940, it was adorned with some 19th-Century jasper and bronze candlesticks from the house of Cheste, which now grace the library stairs.

The chancel is closed by three beautiful screens from the Elorzas' workshops. Their lower storeys were made in 1694 - the pulpits were installed in 1704 - and are by Bartolomé Elorza, the upper storey of the middle screen was wrought by his son Antonio in 1733, and those of the side ones by his successor Gaspar de Aguirre, in 1736.

Among the gilded leafwork crowning them, four medallions are inserted containing the busts of St Engracia and St Geroteo on the right, and St Frutos and St Valentine on the left, from the gouge of Mateo Negrete.

Having visited the chancel, we can begin our walk round the cathedral, in an anticlockwise direction, starting at the Chapel of the Tabernacle.

THE CHAPEL OF THE TABERNACLE

This chapel is made up of two spaces: the old sacristy, by Hontañón, and the chapel as such, at the end.

The old sacristy stands out for its bare architecture decorated with the reredos of the Christ of Agony, popularly known as the Marquis of Lozoya's Christ, as it belonged to that noble Segovian family, who donated it at the end of the last century. The Christ is a 17th-Century piece by the sculptor Manuel de Pereira. For such a beautiful crucifix, Daniel Zuloaga, who had almost just arrived in Segovia, planned the altarpiece surrounding it in 1896, inspired by the ceramics produced by the Della Robbia family, and had the piece fired in "La Segoviana", the old ceramics factory. It was put in place in 1897. The altar front is emblazoned with the arms of Bishop Pozuelo y Herra and of the Lozoyas.

Worthy complements, well within the æsthetics of the moment, are the furniture and the screen, all forged by the local smith Angel Pulido, to Daniel Zuloaga's design.

Opposite the Christ of Agony, there is another reredos, a 17th-Century Baroque one, taken from the old church of St Nicholas, with several paintings from the calendar of saints.

A large arch and two lintelled doorways with two Baroque paintings hanging over them depicting miracles of St Frutos from the circle of the Carduchos (17th Century) lead through to the Chapel of the Tabernacle itself. In 1684, Don Antonio de Ayala y Berganza asked the chapter for a chapel to use as an oratory, reliquary and burial vault. He was granted the back wall of the sacristy, at the time unfinished, and was to spend his large fortune on works on it. The plans are by Juan de Ferreras. In 1686, the height of the first cornice was reached, worked, like the capitals, by Mateo de Escobedo and Andrés de Monasterio. After work was halted on the death of Don Antonio, Juan de Setién Güemes took charge of the work in 1699, committing himself to finishing the dome according to the plan drawn by José de Churriguera. By 1702, the pendentives and the ring of the dome were finished, and in that year Pantaleón Pontón Setién was named master of works, later, because of his ability, to be named master of works of the cathedral. By 1708, it was nearly finished.

The whole chapel is an example of late 17th-Century Castilian Baroque. In 1686, José Benito de Churriguera prepared the plans of the sumptuous reredos, which was to be the first of Spain's so-called Churrigueresque altarpieces. It was made by the reredos specialist Ferreras and the sculptor Bartolomé del Río.

It has a predella, three panels separated by Solomonic columns and a curved pediment with the effigy of St Ferdinand and the shield of the patrons. In the side panels there are niches for reliquaries, while the middle one contains a great monstrance by Antonio Tomé, sheltered by a canopy. This piece, a clear exponent of the Baroque cult of the Holy Sacrament, rests on the Tetramorph, that is the four evangelists in symbolic form. The four sides are adorned with scenes of the Annunciation, Easter, Pentecost and the Lamb of God, alluding to the liturgical calendar: Advent, Easter, Whitsun and ordinary time, which is why it is turned to present the appropriate scene for each cycle. The sides representing the Passion and the Lamb of God may be opened for the display and reserve of the Holy Sacrament. The ensemble is crowned by the image of the Saviour. The piece reached the height of its significance and magnificence on the installation of the Monument to Holy Week, also designed by Daniel Zuloaga, but for some time, the serges, steps, candlesticks and other ornaments that contributed to the religious solemnity have not been displayed.

On the walls are the cenotaphs of four members of the Ayala Berganza family, all members of the cathedral chapter, chiselled by Andrés de Monasterio.

The chapel is enclosed by three screens forged in Vitoria by Martín de Ciorraga and installed in 1762, following the style imposed by the Elorzas.

Facing page, top: *Chancel.*
The Baroque screens enclosing it were forged by Bartolomé Elorza in 1694 and completed by Antonio de Elorza (1733) and Gaspar de Aguirre, a relation of the Elorzas (1736).

Chapel of the Tabernacle. Reredos of the Christ of Agony. The ceramics are by Daniel Zuloaga (1897) and the screen by the Segovian Angel Pulido..

Facing page: *Chapel of the Tabernacle. The Christ of Agony, popularly known as the Marquis of Loyoza's Christ, is a beautiful work by the Baroque sculptor Manuel de Pereira. In the photograph, it is against a velvet background, subsequently removed.*

Little of importance is to be seen in the sacristy and adjoining offices, unlike the archives, where there is a large collection of incunabula. Segovia has the great honour of being Spain's cradle of printing. Indeed, in 1472, the German printer Johannes Parix of Heidelberg, who had come from Subiaco, in Italy, published the *Sinodal de Aguilafuente* ("Synod of Aguilafuente"), named after the nearby village where the synod was held. The typographer came here under the auspices of Bishop Juan Arias Dávila, of *converso* origin (converted from Judaism - *translator's note*), a man of great weight in Segovian culture, and whom we shall have occasion to mention again. Among the examples kept in the archives of work from Parix's presses, special mention should be made of the singular *Expositiones nominum legalium*, in the opinion of Romero de Lecea the first book printed in Spain, and the already mentioned *Sinodal*, real bibliographical jewels and sought after by the most demanding of museums, but inaccessible to the non-specialized public.

In the archives two fine Spanish Baroque canvasses may be admired, depicting St Valentine and St Engracia, and in one of the offices is the Baptism of

Chapel of the Tabernacle.
The old sacristy was designed by Rodrigo Gil de Hontañón and finished in 1572. It is separated from the chapel of the Ayala Berganza family by a screen forged by Martín de Ciorraga (1762). In the left foreground is Manuel de Pereira's 17th-Century sculpture of the Christ of Agony.

Christ, in a small format, reminiscent of the Genoese painter Magnasco. Another two small canvasses of St Barbara and St Frutos, by Bayeu, hang in the corridor and in the antesacristy are the portraits of thirteen bishops of Segovia, most of them from the 18th and 19th Centuries - except the copy of the famous Cobarrubias - among them father Scio, over the entrance to the offices, who died before taking possession of the Diocese.

The present sacristy is very humble and contains nothing worthy of note regarding architecture. It was being decorated in 1747, in which year Manuel Juárez presented the plans for the reredos which was to serve as a frame for the picture of St Charles Borromeo, a copy made in 1796 of Maratti's original given to Charles IV, together with one of Our Lady, on the occasion of a visit made by the monarch, who took a liking to these pictures.

The neo-Classical drawers, for which a plan was drawn by Manuel Andina, were under construction in 1782 and are similar to those of the parish of St Michael.

Having passed through the Renaissance doorway by Rodrigo Gil de Hontañón, we come into a spacious room, a sort of antechapel, on the right wall of which plans exist to place the medieval Calvary from the old cathedral, which is now being repaired. It was once in St Catherine's Chapel and later in the niche on the outside wall of the south arm of the transept.

It follows a pattern that was very common in the Middle Ages, with Christ, the Blessed Virgin and St John, and may be dated in the 13th or 14th Centuries.

We shall start our walk again at St Peter's Chapel.

Chapel of the Tabernacle.
Detail of the reredos. The notable monstrance is an 18th-Century piece by Antonio Tomé. On its front is a relief of the Annunciation and it is topped out by Faith.

ST PETER'S CHAPEL

Before we go on to describe it, a few words should be said about the wall decorations adorning all the chapels off the ambulatory, except St Antón's, which is in keeping with that of the Tabernacle. They were finished well into the 17th Century and dedicated by mutual agreement to the saints, but neither the chapter nor the local gentry were sufficiently well placed financially to meet the cost of furnishing or sponsoring them, so they must have stood unfurnished until the middle of the 18th Century.

By that time, the influence of the Court, set up in the nearby town of La Granja de San Ildefonso, made itself somehow felt in local life. Indeed, Bishop Domingo Valentín Guerra, who was very close to the Court, began in 1737 a chapel dedicated to St Frutos. Although no definite record exists of the date when the present one was painted, we do know that it was furnished in the middle of the century, whence it may be deduced that it was painted shortly afterwards. It is on record that, in 1784, the walls of St Anthony's Chapel, the next one to the left, were decorated *al modo al que se hallan las paredes de la Capilla de San Geroteo*

Preceding double page:

Chapel of the Tabernacle.
The dome was planned by José de Churriguera and finished by Pantaleón Pontón Setién at the beginning of the 18th Century. It rests on pendentives decorated with the busts of the four traditional Segovian saints: St Frutos, St Geroteo, St Valentine and St Engracia, by Andrés de Monasterio (late 17th Century).

("after the fashion of the walls of St Geroteo's Chapel"), which is the next one to the right, having been decorated in 1771. We may therefore conclude that St Frutos's, the central one, on the axis of the ambulatory, was the pattern to be followed by the neighbouring ones, to form a homogeneous whole, in line with Baroque taste. On the wall areas, up to the cornice, an imitation jasper surface has been applied, decorated with garlands, while the rest, up to the vault, is decorated with circular paintings allusive to the saints to whom the chapels are dedicated. The cells of the vaults, among golden ribs, are covered with varied Rococo designs, which afford the circuit of the ambulatory a festive and light-hearted air, so different from the architectural sobriety of the place.

I would assume that, once these chapels were finished, the rest were then done, with the variation of replacing the jasper with imitations of flower-patterned cloths. The model to follow in the four chapels at the ends was changed in the one dedicated to Our Lady of the Rosary, where Bayeu, in order to bring out its Marian significance, decorated all of it with scenes and motifs allusive to the Blessed Virgin.

St Peter's Chapel was founded in the old cathedral, in 1540, by Pedro of Segovia, scribe to King Henry IV. The importance and fame of its chapellany were such that, together with his remains, it was brought to the chapel by the

St Peter's Chapel.
Predella of the reredos with the "Quo Vadis" scene, carved by Pedro de Bolduque in 1585.

Facing page: Chapel of the Tabernacle.
The burial vault of the Ayala Berganza family. The reredos, one of the earliest in the Churrigueresque style, was planned in 1686 by José Benito de Churriguera and carried out by Ferreras and Bartolomé del Río, who made the sculptures.

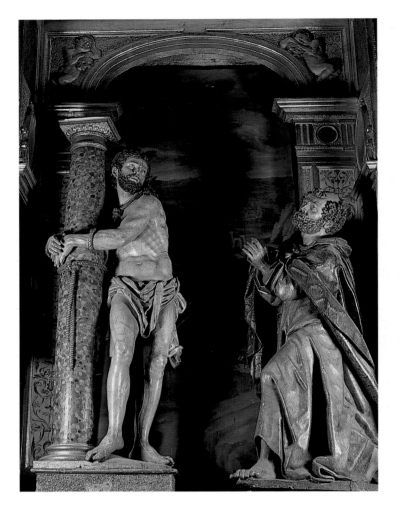

Left: *St Peter's Chapel.*
The reredos, with images of Christ tied to the
Column and of St Peter, was commissioned in
1585 from the sculptor Pedro de Bolduque.

Right: *St Ildefonsus's Chapel.*
The Imposition of the Chasuble on St Ildefonsus
is a subject also to be seen in Toledo Cathedral.
Perhaps it was made by the Segovian Adeba
Pacheco in the 18th Century.

entrance to the cloister of the present cathedral, for which a reredos was commissioned from Pedro de Bolduque in 1585. In 1788, and owing to the inconvenience brought about by the movement of materials for the work on the retrochoir, the reredos and chapellany were set up in the so-called "Chapter of the Well", now St Peter's Chapel, when it was agreed to make a wooden screen.

The reredos, of a single panel, shows on its predella a relief of the subject of *Quo vadis* and in the pediment is a painting of the crucifixion of St Peter by Cristóbal de Velasco (1594-98). The carvings of Christ tied to the column and of St Peter have a Michelangelesque air and are of a high standard.

ST ILDEFONSUS'S CHAPEL

The screen and wall decorations are identical to those of St Peter's Chapel. The reredos, late 18th-Century Classicist Baroque, of stucco'd wood, serves as a frame for the scene of the Imposition of the Chasuble on St Ildefonsus, who, as defender of Mary's virginity, was rewarded by the Blessed Virgin with a magnificent embroidered chasuble which she herself imposed on him, an oft-repeated scene in Spanish art. It is an almost exact replica of the one in Toledo Cathedral. It may have been carved by Adeba Pacheco, as the protégé of Felipe de Castro, sculptor royal and director of the Royal Academy of Fine Arts of St Ferdinand.

Hanging on the walls are two 17th-Century Flemish paintings on copper, a *Noli me tangere* by W. van Herp and "Jesus in the Pool at Bethesda" by P. van Lint.

ST GEROTEO'S CHAPEL

The dedication of this chapel to the first bishop of Segovia, according to tradition, may only be understood in the light of the Baroque taste for legendary founders of bishoprics, well researched in the case in point by R. Cueto.

St Geroteo did not appear in the saints' calendar of Segovia until the 17th Century. According to false chronicles he was present at the Falling Asleep of Mary and was Bishop of Athens, a see he left in order to come and preach in Spain. No less a man than St Paul was to name him Bishop of Segovia. His cult, now defunct, was very popular in Segovia in the Baroque period.

Bishop Juan José Martínez Escalzo, defender of this his spiritual forebear, decided to have himself buried in the cathedral, and the chapter granted him St John's Chapel.

In 1770, the bishop asked for the dedication of the chapel to be changed to the present one and commissioned an elegant reredos from Juan Maurat, the carver of the organ console, the sketch of which, inspired by the reredos in St Frutos's Chapel, but more complicated and Rococo, is preserved in the archives.

In 1771, Manuel Adeba Pacheco finished the sculptures of St Geroteo, St John and St Vincent Ferrer. The tabernacle was decorated with a painting of the Virgin and Child.

On the floor we may see the marble tombstone of the bishop, who died in 1773, the year when the screen forged in Elgóibar by Gregorio de Aguirre was put in place.

Left: St Geroteo's Chapel.
It was funded by Bishop J. Martínez Escalzo and dedicated to St Geroteo, traditionally held to be the first bishop of Segovia. The reredos is by Juan Maurat and the sculpture by Adeba Pacheco, 18th Century.

Right: Ecce Homo. Donated by Bishop Miranda at the beginning of the century for the Holy Week processions.

ST FRUTOS'S CHAPEL

The relics of St Frutos and his brother St Valentine and sister St Engracia, were deposited in a chapel of the south arm of the transept and next to the wall which, until 1684, divided the nave and aisles from the east end. Its demolition entailed that of the chapel. It was then that the present one was dedicated to the Segovian saints. In 1715, Juan de Sierra from Salamanca began a jasper reredos, never to be finished, the plan for which is preserved in the archives.

In 1737, Bishop Domingo Valentín Guerra, confessor to Isabella Farnese and abbot of the collegiate church of La Granja - which might explain the influences of court art in the decoration of the ambulatory chapels - began to build a sumptuous chapel, designed by F. Battista Sachetti, on the outside of the cathedral, next to the *Haceduría* and built onto St Antón's Chapel. When the bishop died in 1742, it could not be built. His heirs, the Marquis and Marchioness of Guerra, faced with the imminent ruin of what had thus far been built, with the consent of the chapter, decided once more to dedicate the central chapel of the ambulatory to St Frutos. In 1747, the three reredoses were ordered, which, together with the carving of the sacristy doors and the wall decorations would enhance the importance deserved by the patron saint of the diocese. In the central reredos we must single out an 18th-Century carving of the Madonna.

Domingo Martínez, who made the reredoses, is also responsible for the screen, installed in 1748.

Opposite the chapel, in the retrochoir wall, is the stone commemorating the consecration of the cathedral to the Assumption of Our Lady and to St Frutos, carried out by Bishop Martínez Escalzo on the 16th July 1748. On either side of it are stones with consecrational crosses with golden horns of plenty underneath them, motifs repeated in the arms of the transept and on the west face.

ST ANTHONY'S CHAPEL

The reredos, donated by an anonymous worshipper in 1782, is similar to, but simpler than, St Geroteo's, although the elimination of the side niches, together with the use of a marble-like stucco rather than gold, reflect the taste of the times for purging the arts. It is presided over by an image of the saint himself, flanked by a Jesuit saint and a St Teresa, the last made of paste and modern, probably put there in place of the figure of St Alfonso Rodríguez, a Segovian Jesuit, which is now on the retable of St Engracia's reredos, in the previous chapel.

In 1784, the same worshipper financed the painting of the walls. Among the canvasses on them, an Immaculate Conception by Bayeu is worthy of note.

THE CHAPEL OF OUR LADY OF THE ROSARY

The simple reredos frames a canvass of Our Lady of the Rosary, dated and signed by Don Ramón Bayeu in 1789. Perhaps the frescoes on the walls may be attributed to the same painter and, as has already been said, they break the strict symmetry of decoration kept to in the other chapels. On the lower part, in circles, groups of angels extol the rosary. Higher up, on the sections of wall between the cornice and the vault are two Marian scenes: on the left, the Blessed Virgin with St Joachim and St Anne; and on the right, the Holy Family with St Elizabeth and the young St John.

In the floor is the tombstone of a curious "venerable" lady of Segovia, María Quintana, whose portrait hangs on the wall.

The chapel is closed in by an elegant neo-Classical bronze screen designed by the academician Alfonso Rodríguez in 1795, although the finishing pieces and the bishop's shield are missing.

Top: St Frutos's Chapel.
St Valentine's reredos, a mid-18th-Century piece by Domingo Martínez.

Facing page: St Frutos's Chapel.
Funded by the wish of Bishop Valentín Guerra. The reredoses are of the saint to whom it is dedicated and St Valentine and St Engracia. They were decided on in 1747.

Bottom: St Frutos's Chapel.
Reredos of St Engracia, a mid-18th-Century piece by Domingo Martínez.

Top: *St Anthony's Chapel.*
Image of the saint, an anonymous carving of the
18th Century.

Chapel of Our Lady of the Rosary.
The canvass was painted by Ramón Bayeu in
1789 and is an example of an art popular in court
circles and which left several testimonies in the
cathedral.

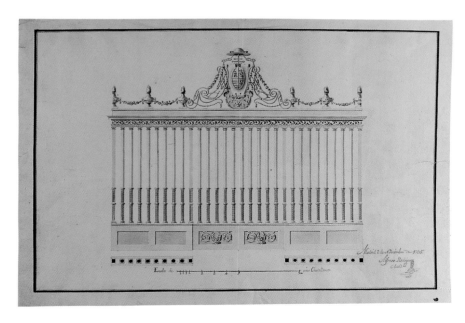

Chapel of Our Lady of the Rosary.
The neo-Classical bronze screen was designed by
Alfonso Rodríguez in 1795. The drawing is
preserved in the archives.

ST JOSEPH'S CHAPEL

It is the simplest and humblest one in the cathedral. In October 1791, Bishop Francisco Jiménez showed the chapter the plan for the reredos. We must remember that the high altar had recently been consecrated, and that it was highly regarded at the time, so it was doubtless used as a model, as St Joseph's reredos is designed along similar lines. It its central niche is the image of St Joseph and in the pediment are those of St Teresa and St John of the Cross, Carmelite saints having strong links with local history, accompanying a relief of St John the Baptist, the three on white-painted wood. They may be by Manuel Adeba Pacheco.

Certain details permit us to link this reredos with J. Ortega's in the chapter-house.

Chapel of Our Lady of the Rosary.
Angels carrying Marian motifs, an fresco by
Ramón Bayeu, late 18th Century.

ST ANTÓN'S CHAPEL

In 1615 the chapter granted Don Antonio Idiáquez Múgica, a member of a noble family and bishop of Segovia, a chapel for his burial, but it was not to be furnished until the end of the century.

In 1695 the reredos was drawn by José Vallejo Vivanco, the notable maker of reredoses and master of royal works, who finished it in 1697. It consists of a predella, adorned with the arms of the Múgica and Idiáquez families, a main storey and a curious topping which takes in the Gothic windows. Four Solomonic columns divide the corpus into three panels, the central one with the statue of St Antón, by the sculptor Pedro Valle (1706) and the side ones with two paintings by Francisco Herranz, the cathedral's famous glazier, depicting two miracles by St Frutos: the stabbing, and the sieve with the consecrated Host.

To the left we may contemplate the most ornate tomb in the cathedral. It was begun in 1712 and a year later the sculptor José Galván finished the figure of the young bishop at prayer and those of the page boys started by Pedro Valle. The whole was to be painted white in the middle of the century.

The silver lamp was made by the Segovian goldsmith Bartolomé Moreno in 1714.

The chapel is enclosed by a screen made by Antonio de Elorza, installed in 1729 and gilded in 1755.

The cathedral is an excellent showcase of Baroque screen-making, most of it forged in Elgóibar by the Elorza family. The screen of St Antón's Chapel was funded by Bishop Idiáquez, whose arms crown it. It was made by Antonio de Elorza (1729).

Facing page: St Antón's Chapel.
Bishop Idiáquez's tomb, the most ornate in the whole church, was begun in 1712 by Pedro Valle and completed by José Galván.

This page: *St Antón's Chapel.*
The reredos was planned in 1695 by José Vallejo Vivanco, who made
other notable ones in the city. The image of St Antón is
by Pedro Valle (1706).

Facing page: *Chapels off the ambulatory.*
Finished at the beginning of the 17th Century, they were decorated and
furnished some time into the 18th, with influence of the style developed in
the nearby palace of La Granja.

Chapel of the Pietà.
*The Blessed Virgin and St John, a detail of
Christ's Burial, by Juan de Juni, 16th Century.*

Facing page: *Chapel of the* Pietà.
*The reredos of Christ's Burial was made by Juan
de Juni in 1571. In the centre is a high relief with
the Blessed Virgin, St John, Salome, Mary
Magdalen, Nicodemus and Joseph of Arimathæa.
In the intercolumns there are soldiers, and the
piece is crowned by a medallion containing the
Eternal Father.*

Following double page:

Chapel of the Pietà.
*Christ's Burial. Around the figure of Christ, from
left to right: Nicodemus, Salome, the Blessed
Virgin, St John, Mary Magdalen and Joseph of
Arimathæa.*

THE CHAPEL OF THE *PIETÀ*

This was the first chapel granted to an individual, in this case to Juan Rodríguez, the famous canon and treasurer, who acquired it in 1551. In this way the chapter recognized the watchfulness of the canon, who from 1522 until 1562, when he drew up the report allowing us to follow the history of the building of the cathedral, had been in charge of the "government of the fabric and works". There is, however, no stone to his memory, unless it is buried under the altar.

The chapel houses two masterpieces of sculpture and painting. The reredos, with a high relief of the Holy Burial, is one of the most outstanding pieces by Juan de Juni, who carved it in 1571. At the feet of the Blessed Virgin and St John, both overcome by pain, is the body of Christ, whose head is held up by Joseph of Arimathæa. Above him, Salome extends her headdress towards Nicodemus, who, at Christ's feet, by repeating the gesture with his veil, rounds off the elliptical shape of this very tight composition, in which there is barely space for Mary Magdalen, who, with great difficulty, opens up a gap to behold the recumbent form.

The quality of the carving, the pathos and the polychromy go together to make this a masterpiece of Spanish sculpture.

The Eternal Father and the soldiers between the columns do not detract from the central group. The reredos is complemented by paintings of angels holding up motifs of the Passion, by Santos Pedril (1571).

Chapel of the Pietà.
It was granted to the verger Juan Rodríguez in 1551. The screen, brought here from the chancel of the old cathedral, was forged by Friar Francisco of Salamanca in 1506. It is crowned by a Calvary scene and has the apostles Peter, Paul, James and Andrew at the sides.

Preceding double page:

Chapel of the Pietà.
The Triptych of the Taking Down by the Flemish painter Ambrosius Benson, painted around 1532-36, is one of the most important works of art in the cathedral. In the centre, the Taking Down. On the left, St Michael and on the right, St Anthony. It came here from the parish of St Michael.

Opposite is the Triptych of the Taking Down - one of the largest Flemish paintings of the 16th Century - by the Flemish painter Ambrosius Benson, inspired by another by Robert Campin, and which must have been painted around 1532-36.

In the central panel the dead Christ is taken down from the cross by Joseph of Arimathæa, who holds His trunk, and by Nicodemus, who holds His legs. At His feet, Mary Magdalen and another person come to help. To the left, Mary, held up by St John and overwhelmed by sorrow, holds her hands out towards her Son. She is accompanied by Salome and Mary the wife of Clopas. To the right, two richly attired men contemplate the scene. At the top is a group of angels.

On the side panels are St Anthony against a picturesque landscape, and St Michael, somewhat reminiscent of Leonardo.

The triptych comes from the neighbouring church of St Miguel, which is why it has no connexion, contrary to what one might think, with the reredos of which it is the iconographic antecedent.

A worthy complement is the beautiful screen, which, brought from the old cathedral, was given by the chapter to the chapel as a token of thanks for the work that the treasurer had successfully brought about. It was forged at the beginning of the 16th Century by Friar Francisco of Salamanca.

St Andrew's Chapel.
The reredos was designed by the Segovian
architect Pedro de Brizuela in 1621 and was
completed in 1623. Felipe de Aragón carved the
statue of the saint and the relief of his
martyrdom, the remaining sculptures being by
Juan Imberto.

ST ANDREW'S CHAPEL

Canon Andrés de Madrigal having founded the chapel in 1620, one year later, the plan was drawn by the architect Pedro de Brizuela for the reredos. It was finished in 1623 and gilded in 1703.

It has two storeys, plus a pediment, is in three panels and is carved throughout. Juan Imberto carved the figures of St Peter, St Paul and the evangelists St Luke and St John on the lower storey, which are matched by those of St Mark and St Matthew on the upper one. Felipe de Aragón carved the figure of the saint to whom the chapel is dedicated and the relief of his martyrdom on the pediment.

For the screen, inspired by the one in St James's Chapel, plans were drawn in 1621 by Francisco Hernández, from Madrid, but the screen we see today is by the Sánchez brothers of Salamanca, and was installed in 1633.

The fact that it was inspired by the one in St James's Chapel, the one opposite, and that the rest of screens match each other exactly, including those by Friar Francisco of Salamanca, but with the exceptions of those of the chapels of St Blasius and the Conception, leads me to think in terms of an ordered plan for all of them.

*Above: Chapel of St Cosmas and St Damian.
17th-Century Madonna from the circle of
Gregorio Fernández.*

*Chapel of St Cosmas and St Damian.
In 1631, Gregorio Fernández signed the contract
for the effigies of the saints, although they are
considered to be atelier pieces.*

THE CHAPEL OF ST COSMAS AND ST DAMIAN

It was granted to Damián Alonso Berrocal, whose arms emblazon the altarpiece, screen and tombstones.

In 1621, the reredos was mooted but it was not to be finished until 1631, by Domingo Fernández. Though in that year the famous sculptor Gregorio Fernández signed a contract to make the figures of St Cosmas and St Damian and an Immaculate Conception, it is known that by his death they had not been delivered, so they are at best considered as atelier pieces.

The wall is adorned with a grisaille triptych of the Immaculate Conception with St Cosmas and St Damian made at the beginning of the 17th Century and, in the opinion of Collar de Cáceres, within the style of Cristóbal de Velasco.

The screen was wrought by Antonio de Elorza and installed in 1738.

ST GREGORY'S CHAPEL

It is the foundation of Alonso Nieto and his wife, who bought it in 1623.

The reredos, late 17th-Century, may be by Vallejo Vivanco, as it has some similarities with St Antón's. Its three panels, divided by Solomonic columns, bear

Chapel of the Conception.
The Immaculate Conception is by the sculptor
Antonio de Herrera, from Madrid, and is dated
1621.

canvasses of the Imposition of the Chasuble on St Ildefonsus, St Gregory's Mass and St Michael. The pediment has an Assumption, almost a rule of the moment.

The Baroque screen, with the arms of the patrons, is by Antonio de Elorza and was installed in 1716.

THE CHAPEL OF THE CONCEPTION

In 1606 the chapter decided to decorate the first chapel by the west door of the cathedral and the one opposite, or St Blasius's. Shortly afterwards, in 1620, the Spanish church became a vehement supporter of the Immaculate Conception, which dogma would be taken on by the Vatican in 1854. The Segovia chapter also defended the idea and in 1621 commissioned a carving of the Immaculate Conception from Antonio de Herrera, which would be ready a year later, when the ribs of the vault were gilded.

In 1645, the chapel was given to the trusteeship of Pedro Fernández de Miñano y Contreras, who had several important posts in Andalusia, and who justifies the presence of six canvasses by Ignacio de Ries, a disciple of Zurbarán, duly signed and dated. The chapel is literally covered in paintings of scenes of the life of the Blessed Virgin, culminating in one of her Coronation on the reredos, where the painter takes advantage of Herrera's beautiful sculpture to involve it in the scene. This extolling of Mary, which the chapter was committed to defend on

Following double page:

Left: *Chapel of the Conception.*
The Baptism of Christ, by Ignacio de Ries of
Seville (1653).

Right: *Chapel of the Conception.*
The Tree of Life, by Ignacio de Ries, dated 1653,
is an allusion to the transience of earthly
pleasure and the imminence of death.

oath, in the "pure Conception of Mary" also accounts for the motifs painted in the cells of the vault and the alleluias over some of the pictures. The relationship with Mary is not, however, so direct in four of the six paintings by Ries (the one of David was painted by him in 1653 in Seville) adorning the lower part: the Baptism of Christ, the Tree of Life, the Conversion of St Paul and King David, while it is in the two smaller ones on either side of the reredos: the Coronation and the Adoration of the Shepherds.

Because of its singularity, special mention should be made of the Allegory of the Tree of Life, very much in keeping with the religious mentality of the Counter-Reformation. Death fells the tree in whose crown a merry group of people are enjoying the pleasures of life without hearing the sound of the bell being rung by Christ announcing the imminence of death.

Don Pedro's status as an admiral is alluded to by the ships painted on the wall. The chapel is closed by a curious wooden screen, made before 1645.

THE RETROCHOIR

In 1782, the chapter, faced with the deplorable appearance of the retrochoir, asked Charles III for the marble reredos in the chapel at the Riofrío Palace, not inhabited, which the king granted.

The reredos had been made by Hubert Dumandre in 1758, but only the central panel existed, so it was necessary to add wings to it for it to take up the whole width of the nave between the pillars. The first artist considered was J. Dumandre, Hubert's son, but opinions offered led Floridablanca to propose that Juan de Villanueva should draw up a plan in 1783, this plan being kept to by his successors in the undertaking: Ventura Rodríguez and Juan de la Torre y López. The work was very slow and fraught with contrasting opinions, and was not to be over until 1789, when Estévez finished off the pediment on the choir side.

The reredos has a central corpus containing a niche where, in a silver urn made by Sebastián de Paredes in 1633, the relics of St Frutos are venerated. The ensemble is crowned by sculptures of St Peter, St Paul and the Holy Trinity. To the sides are the images of St Philip and St Elizabeth, in memory of the king's parents, Philip V and Isabella* Farnese, by court painters, their precise identity being the subject of some dispute.

The sides of the choir were made by the local architect Juan de la Torre y López, who faithfully followed Villanueva's plans. They are of stucco'd wood, with statues in white-painted wood of the evangelists, attributed to Manuel Adeba Pacheco, in the niches.

The chapel is protected by a simple screen forged by the Segovian Félix Egido in 1793.

In front of this reredos, the counterpoint in many ways of the one behind the High Altar, a very popular *villancico* is sung every 25th October, on St Frutos's Day.

It is now time to say a few words about St Frutos, a saint we have seen on the main door, in the Chancel, in the chapel named after him, etc. Tradition has it that this Visigothic saint was born in Segovia and retired, in the company of his brother Valentine and sister Engracia to the loneliness of the Duratón gorges, where, in an almost inaccessible place, he died in 715. His life dedicated to prayer and penitence, he founded a priory which became part of the monastery of St Dominic of Silos. The present church was consecrated in 1100.

At the other end from the retrochoir is the sober interior of the west face, where the church's consecrational crosses are accompanied by horns of plenty and four Baroque paintings of scenes from the life of the Spanish Augustinian saint Tomás de Villanueva (1486-1555). This saint from La Mancha, known as the *Father of the Poor*, for the love he showed to the needy, entered St Ildefonsus's College in Alcalá de Henares in 1508. From there he went to

*Isabella and Isabel are, respectively, the Italian and Spanish equivalents of Elizabeth - *translator's note*.

Facing page: *Chapel of the Conception.*
The Spanish church's defence of the dogma of the Immaculate Conception was made manifest in the cathedral in a chapel, whose vault it decorated with Marian symbols.

Chapel of the Conception.
The ships allude to the chapel patron's status as an admiral.

Salamanca, where he took the habit of the Augustinians, despite being asked to become a lecturer at the University (1516). Preacher and adviser to Charles V, he was named Archbishop of Valencia (1544), where he carried out a great deal of apostolic and social work. He was canonized in 1658.

The four late 17th-Century Baroque canvasses narrate from left to right the exposition of the Holy Scriptures in Salamanca, entering St Ildefonsus's College led by Cardinal Cisneros, his asceticism and love for the poor.

In the centre is a beautiful painting of Our Lady of Antigua, from the end of the 16th Century or beginning of the 17th - perhaps Cornelio Martín's painting that Collar de Cáceres mentions? Finally, on the mullion there is an exquisite Gothic sculpture of Our Lady of Pardon.

This page: *Urn containing the remains of St Frutos, by the silversmith Sebastián de Paredes, 1633.*

Facing page: *The Retrochoir.*
In 1758, Hubert Dumandre made the central corpus, previously in the chapel of Riofrío Palace. In 1783, Juan de Villanueva planned its removal to the cathedral. In the work, not concluded until 1789, parts were taken by Ventura Rodríguez and Estévez.

Top left: *Retrochoir.*
St Matthew, a wooden sculpture by M. Adeba
Pacheco, late 18th Century.

Top right: *Retrochoir.*
St Luke, a wooden image by M. Adeba Pacheco,
late 18th Century.

Bottom left: *Doorway of Pardon.*
The image of Our Lady, brought from the old
cathedral, presides over the mullion and is the
only sculpture on this face of the cathedral.

Bottom right: *West Doorway.*
Our Lady of Pardon, on the mullion of the thus-
named doorway, a wood carving and one of the
few medieval Marian images in the cathedral.

ST BLASIUS'S CHAPEL

It is the first one on the Epistle side. It serves as an access to the tower stairs. Though the chapel is dedicated to St Blasius, its late 17th-Century Baroque reredos may not have been made exactly for the place it is in. It is presided over by the saint, accompanied by paintings of two Fathers of the Church and, in the pediment, a picture alluding to his miracle working powers. Perhaps it would be pushing things a little to suppose a link between the dedication of this chapel - together with the bell tower - to St Blasius with his patronship of wind instrument musicians. What there is no doubt about is the presence of music in the images of St Cecilia and King David, which is why until recently the city's musicians honoured their patron saint in this chapel.

The most interesting piece is the screen, made in the 16th Century, on whose lock the arms of the Fonseca family, lords of the town of Coca, tell us of it origin. It was in fact brought here from Coca parish church at the end of the 18th Century.

St Blasius's Chapel.
One of the cathedral's humblest Baroque reredoses, with the saint in the centre.

CHAPEL OF THE TAKING DOWN

This chapel, also known as the Chapel of the Sepulchre, was acquired by Canon Cristóbal Bernaldo de Quirós in 1661. The 17th-Century Baroque reredos follows the tradition of the Ferreras altarpieces and is an eloquent testimony of Christ's Passion, the sequence of which - Death, Taking Down and Burial - is shown on the central panel. The painting on the pediment of the Crucifixion and the one in the centre of the Taking Down were done by Francisco Camilo from Madrid in the 17th Century. The Baroquism of the canvasses contrasts with the serenity of the Dead Christ, until recently on the predella and now on the altar table, to lend weight to the sacrifice of the Eucharist, as was preceptive. The rest of the statues and paintings refer clearly to the Passion. The Recumbent Christ, a singular work by Gregorio Fernández, a 17th-Century Castilian master craftsman, with its carefully studied anatomy and colouring, is an exact reflection of popular piety, which seeks for a prop for its faith in things natural.

*Chapel of the Taking Down.
The mid-17th-Century Baroque reredos serves as a frame for the pictures by the Madrid painter Francisco Camilo: the Crucifixion and the Taking Down, which, together with Gregorio Fernández's Recumbent Christ, manifest Our Lord's sacrifice.*

Facing and following pages:

*Chapel of the Taking Down:
On the predella of the reredos is the beautiful sculpture of the Recumbent Christ, a masterpiece by Gregorio Fernández, of the Valladolid School, 17th Century.*

82

Details of Gregorio Fernández's Recumbent Christ, of an extraordinary expressiveness and a faithful reflection of Baroque piety.

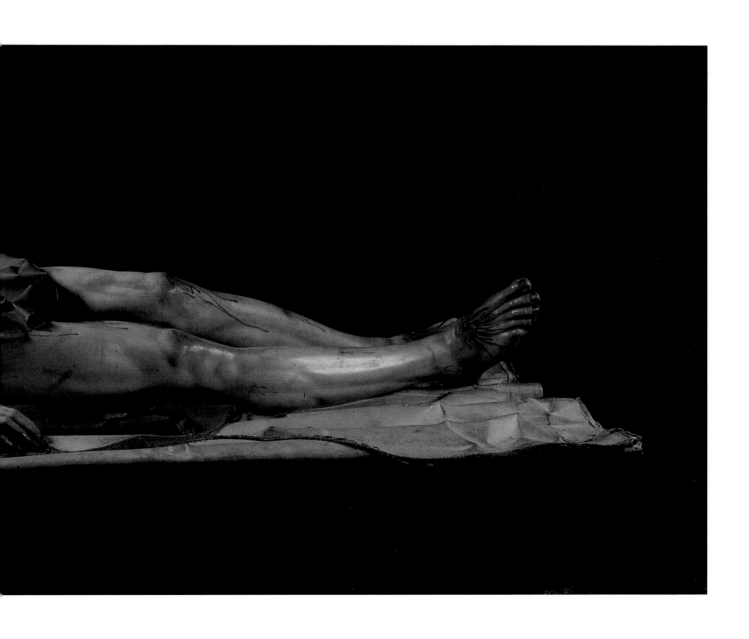

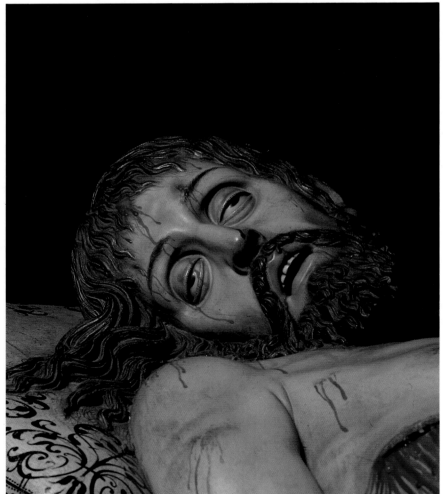

St Barbara's Chapel.
Detail of the baptismal font, with the shield of
Castile and Henry IV's emblem.

ST BARBARA'S CHAPEL

It is used as a parish church, whence the Gothic baptismal font, brought here from the old cathedral, and adorned with the arms of Castile and León together with pomegranates, the emblem of Henry IV.

The reredos, made of stone, must have been made by Pedro de Brizuela at the beginning of the 17th Century, commissioned by some member of the church, whose shields, without arms, are to be seen at the sides.

It closely follows the arrangement of the upper storey of St Frutos's doorway and although the Ionic order may seem somewhat suspicious, we should remember that Brizuela used one on the west doorway of St Sebastian's parish church at Villacastín.

In 1788 it was stucco'd to resemble marble, which gives it a strange Classicist Baroque appearance. The image of St Barbara belongs to the same century.

The screen, installed in 1741, is by Gregorio de Aguirre.

ST JAMES'S CHAPEL

It was acquired in 1577 by Don Francisco Gutiérrez de Cuéllar, Head Accountant to Philip II and minister of his Treasury Council.

The reredos was made by Pedro de Bolduque in 1591 and dedicated to St James. It comprises a predella, with a relief of the moving of the apostle's body and the portrait and arms of the founder. In the corpus is a carving of St James and on the lateral panels are "St James's Calling" and "St James's Martyrdom", on canvass. The upper storey shows a high relief of St James the Slayer of Moors. The altarpiece is completed by other sculptures and reliefs and the Cross of the Order of St James. The paintings are by Alonso de Herrera. No little doubt exists, however, as to who painted Gutiérrez de Cuéllar's portrait, on occasions attributed to him, though its quality would put it nearer to Sánchez Coello. At the end of the chapel a granite doorway gives access to the so-called sacristy, which is in fact a crypt, planned in 1589 by Rodrigo de Solar. The screen was made by Juan de Salamanca in the 1690s.

Top: St Barbara's Chapel.
Baptismal font, 15th-Century Gothic, with the arms of Castile and León and the emblem of Henry IV, brought from the old cathedral.

Bottom:
St James's Chapel.
The Removal of St James's body, on the altarstep, by Pedro de Bolduque (1591).

CHAPEL OF THE CHRIST OF SOLACE

Like so many other churches and cathedrals, Segovia Cathedral had a chapel dedicated to Christ Crucified in the retrochoir, until, owing to the installation of the Riofrío reredos, it was transferred here.

The simple Baroque reredos bears the image of Christ, dressed in a kirtle, brought here from the Jesuit School. It is a Baroque piece of the 17th Century. Opposite it are the tombs of the first Archbishop of Seville, the Segovian Don Raimundo de Losana, and the Bishop of Segovia Don Diego de Covarrubias, son of the famous architect. Over the little doorway leading to a spiral staircase there is a 15th-Century stone *Pietà*, brought here from the gate of the Canonjías quarter.

The chapel is closed by the choir screen from the old cathedral, forged by Friar Francisco of Salamanca in 1508.

Chapel of the Christ of Solace.
The effigy of Christ is a Baroque sculpture of the 17th Century, dressed in a popular kirtle.

Facing page:

Top left: *St James's Chapel.*
Image of the saint by the sculptor Pedro de Bolduque (1591).

Top right: *St James's Chapel.*
High relief of the image of St James "the Slayer of Moors", by Pedro de Bolduque (1591).

Bottom: *St James's Chapel.*
The ribs and cells were gilded and painted at the end of the 16th Century or beginning of the 17th, thus beginning a custom which would culminate in the chapels off the ambulatory. Frescoes with Renaissance motifs are rather rare in Segovia, which makes them interesting.

CLOISTER AND MUSEUM

From the Chapel of the Christ of Solace, the cloister is reached through a splendid doorway, also brought here from the demolished Cathedral of St Mary and emplaced here at the beginning of the 16th Century.

It was paid for by Isabel the Catholic and planned by Juan Guas in 1483. In 1486 the architectural work was finished and the sculpture was commissioned from Sebastián de Almonacid. It is presided over from the tympanum by the Fifth Sorrow surrounded by angels holding the instruments of the Passion. On the left-hand jamb are figures of St Peter and St Paul, with St James and St John the Baptist on the right-hand one. Over the tympanum is the shield of Castile with the eagle of St John - the royal emblem - and crowning the whole are the figures of St Bartholomew, St John, St Thomas and St Andrew. The figures were last retouched in 1764 by Manuel de Quintanilla.

Though less exuberant, the decoration on the inside of the doorway is also quite delicate. The tympanum shows the Annunciation, and the archivolts bear the Visit at St Elizabeth's, the Flight to Egypt, the Presentation and the Birth. At the top is Veronica. The whole is painted white, except for the hands and heads.

Now the beautiful cloister opens up before our eyes, thanks to the munificence of Bishop Juan Arias Dávila, who commissioned it from Juan Guas in 1471. It has a square groundplan and simple vaulting, except in the eastern walk, where the bosses bear sculptures of the Coronation of the Blessed Virgin, Arias Dávila's arms (eagle, castle and cross), a shield (?) and the symbols of the Passion.

The moving of the cloister and doorway, successfully carried out by the architectural technician Juan Campero in 1530, has been considered by ancients and moderns alike as a feat worthy of admiration.

At the beginning of the walk running parallel to the aisles there are three granite tombstones of masters of works, brought here from their original setting at the end of the 18th Century, when the cloister was paved. The middle one, made in 1620, belongs to Rodrigo Gil, who died in 1577; the one on the left is that of Francisco de Campo Agüero (d. 1660), and the one on the right is Francisco Viadero's (d. 1688).

During the Baroque period, the bottoms of the windows were blocked up with a simple parapet, perhaps because the bases of the mullions were in bad condition. At the end of the 19th Century, Joaquín de Odriozola returned them to their original state and designed the gateway to the garden.

Facing page: Chapel of the Christ of Solace.
Doorway of the cloister, by Juan Guas and the sculptor Sebastián de Almonacid, late 15th Century. The tympanum shows a Pietà *and the piece is crowned with the arms of the Catholic Monarch, who funded it.*

This page: Cloister.
Chapel of the Cabrera (?) family, by Juan Guas, removed from the old cathedral by Juan Campero between 1525 and 1529.

93

Above: *Chapel of the Christ of Solace.*
Sebastián de Almoncid's Pietà *relief on the tympanum of the cloister*
doorway. The original polychromy of this 15th-Century piece has been
repainted several times.

Facing page:

Top: *Cloister.*
The cloister was planned by Juan Guas and moved to its present site by
Juan Campero in 1525.

Bottom left: *The garden boasts some impressive box trees.*

Bottom centre: *This little neo-Gothic gateway is 19th-Century.*

Bottom right: *North walk, roofed with simple ribbed vaults.*

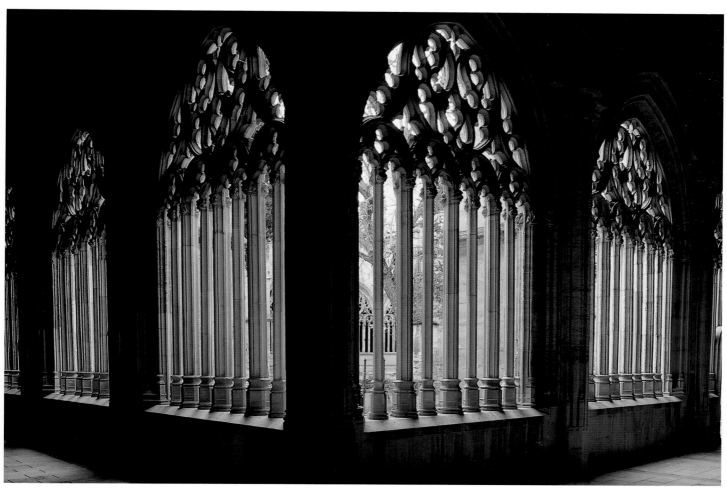

THE MUSEUM

St Catherine's Chapel, the bottom storey of the tower, is used as the Cathedral museum. In the centre is the tomb of Prince Peter, son of Henry II, whose untimely death occurred in the *Alcázar* in 1366.

As a chapel, it has an altar, and in it cult was rendered, until the 19th Century, to the beautiful Gothic Calvary scene, brought from the old cathedral. In 1857 it was taken to the niche in the south arm of the transept.

Paintings, tapestries, sculptures and other objets d'art are displayed on the walls and in showcases. Among the sculptures is a 13th-Century Madonna and Child and a curious Pantocrator, a 15th-Century piece, old-fashioned for its time, with the following inscription on its plinth: *Esta obra manda faser el cura de Fernan Muñoz beneficiado en esta dicha yglesia* ("This piece was commissioned by the priest of Fernán Muñoz, beneficiary of this church").

Regarding the paintings, and beginning on the right, we have "St Thomas's Doubt" painted on board in 1585 by Alonso Sánchez Coello, the painter to whom the portrait in St James's Chapel is attributed, a curious copy of Van Eyck's "Fountain of Grace" which was in the monastery of El Parral; over the altar is "St Gregory's Mass" by Pedro Berruguete (16th Century), the 16th-Century Flemish triptych "The Virgin and Child" with St Catherine and St Barbara, by the Master of the Holy Blood; a small Renaissance altarpiece; the Holy Trinity, a 15th-Century painting on board by the Segovian Master of the Carnations, and a very curious Madonna and Child, monumentally executed by an Italian painter whose identity is in doubt, though on the frame we can make out "...o de Biterbo" - perhaps Andrea Mariotto de Viterbo?; and lastly, a fine painting of Christ tied to the Column, a 16th-Century picture by Morales, until recently kept in St Gregory's Chapel.

Triptych of the Virgin and Child, attributed to the Master of the Holy Blood and painted in the first quarter of the 16th Century. The lateral panels show St Catherine and St Barbara.

Facing page: St John, detail from the Calvary scene brought from the old cathedral. It is a wooden figure from the 13th or 14th century and one of the few movable objects saved from the destruction of the original cathedral of St Mary.

97

This page: Left: *Wood carving of Christ blessing, of unknown origin. 14th Century.*

Right: *Consecrational sacring tablet, made about 1575.*

Facing page:

Top left: *St Thomas's Doubt, by Alonso Sánchez Coello, 1585.*

Top right: *Silver sceptre with top resembling a building. A singular work of the silversmith Alvaro, dated between 1491 and 1494.*

Bottom left: *15th-Century silver-gilt and rock crystal processional cross. The plinth is Baroque and was made in 1656.*

Bottom centre: *Ivory figure of Christ, 17th Century.*

Bottom right: *Silver and gold-on-bronze candlesticks. They belong to the three pairs made by Antonio F. Venedetti.*

The showcases contain silver objects of liturgical use. Segovia, like other cities, had good silversmiths, and many of the pieces on show here are by them. The first cabinet contains a 16th-Century rock crystal altar cross, possibly German, a sacring tablet of the Consecration, in the shape of a small altarpiece, with several different scenes, the quality of which used to lead experts to think it may have been made by Cellini. It was made about 1775. The silver-gilt and rock crystal processional cross is 16th Century, with a Baroque base made in 1656. On the lower shelf are two Baroque pieces: a sacring tablet of the Consecration, from the second half of the 18th Century, and a portable stoup made about 1744. Among the items in the second case are, on the top shelf, a silver-gilt tabernacle (18th Century), a silver ciborium (late 16th or early 17th Century), two mid-18th-Century chalices and, on the middle shelf, a mid-18th-Century silver lectern and a 15th-Century Evangeliary with a silver cover.

The third cabinet houses two silver sceptres, made about 1491-94, some Baroque croziers, two 16th-Century silver candlesticks and three silver jars for Holy Oils, made in 1753.

In the fourth case there are several ivory figures of Christ, reliquaries, trays and jugs of the 18th Century. Along the wall are the tall bronze candlesticks made by Vendetti, to Sabatini's design (1771-73), which once stood in the Chancel.

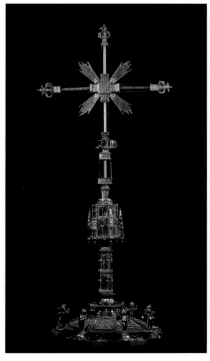

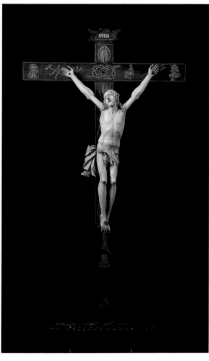

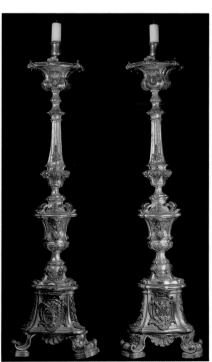

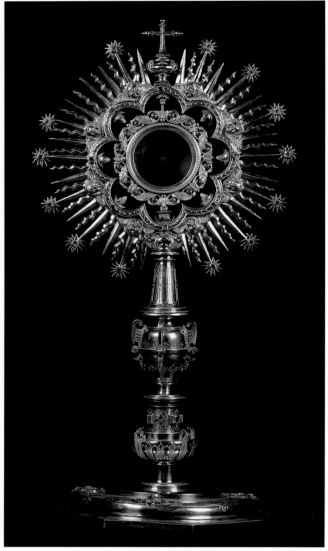

Top left: *Museum.*
Tabernacle by the goldsmith Rafael González.
Gilded bronze, mid 17th Century.

Top right: *Silver-gilt tabernacle by the goldsmith*
Ignacio Alvarez Arintero, made in the second half
of the 18th Century.

Bottom: *Velvet and silver lectern, by Baltasar de*
Salazar, 18th Century, with the arms of Bishop
García Medrano. On the right is an Evangeliary
with a cover in silver, velvet and enamel, showing
the Maiestas Domini, *15th Century.*

Top: *Three pieces of precious metalwork. From left to right, a late 16th-Century silver-gilt ciborium, a silver-gilt chalice from the first half of the 18th Century and a gilded bronze ciborium from the first half of the 17th Century.*

Bottom: *Two pieces of Baroque precious metalwork. An altar lamp and a portable stoup, the latter made by José Nájera and dated 1714.*

This page: *Chapter-house.
Built under the direction of García de Cubillas,
mid 16th Century.*

Facing page: *The Chapter-house is hung with a set
of tapestries woven in Brussels by Geeraert
Peemans in the 17th Century, which tell the story
of Zenobia, Queen of Palmyra.*

Preceding pages:

Left-hand page:
Top left: *Museum. The tomb of Prince Pedro, son
of Henry II, whom tradition holds to have fallen
from one of the balconies of the Alcázar in 1366.*
Top right: *French tapestry with scene of gallantry.
17th Century.*

Bottom left: *In St Catherine's Chapel hangs this
impressive painting, previously in St Gregory's
Chapel, painted by Luis de Morales at the end of
the 16th Century.*

Bottom right: *Madonna and Child, painted on
board. Possibly Italian. Early 16th Century.*

Right-hand page: *Detail of a French tapestry with
a scene of gallantry. 17th Century.*

The walls are adorned with French tapestries showing scenes of gallantry. One fine piece is the altarcloth for the mass for the dead, decorated with the arms of the House of Austria.

The second part of the museum is in the old library and Chapter House. This room, whose coffering was made by the master carpenter Francisco López in 1599, was decorated in the 18th Century, when the coffering and walls were painted, the former gold and white, and the Classicist Baroque reredos was commissioned from the carver José Ortega, to house José Esteve's "Conception", also 18th Century. On the altar table are three silver sacring tablets, the lateral ones made in 1769 and the central one about ten years later. The walls are completely covered with tapestries showing the Story of Queen Zenobia, woven in Brussels by Geeraert Peemans in the 17th Century. At the end, under a canopy, is a 17th-Century figure of Christ, which used to stand in the Chapel of the Conception.

At the foot of the stairs hangs a canvass by Carlos María Esquivel, painted in 1862 and showing Charles V and St Francis Borgia in Yuste, and the portrait of Don Antonio de Ayala, founder of the Chapel of the Tabernacle, painted by José García Hidalgo in 1686.

The piece that most attracts the visitor's attention is without a doubt, the triumphal carriage and silver tabernacle, which is taken out in procession through the streets of the city to celebrate Corpus Christi. The tabernacle, made along traditional lines in imitation of a building, was fashioned by the Madrid goldsmith Rafael González, who worked on it from 1653 to 1657, the dates on the piece. All the figures and decoration serve to extol the Holy Sacrament.

The tabernacle rests on an exquisite 18th-Century Baroque carriage, made of gilded wood, with the small front wheels hidden under hanging drapes. It seems

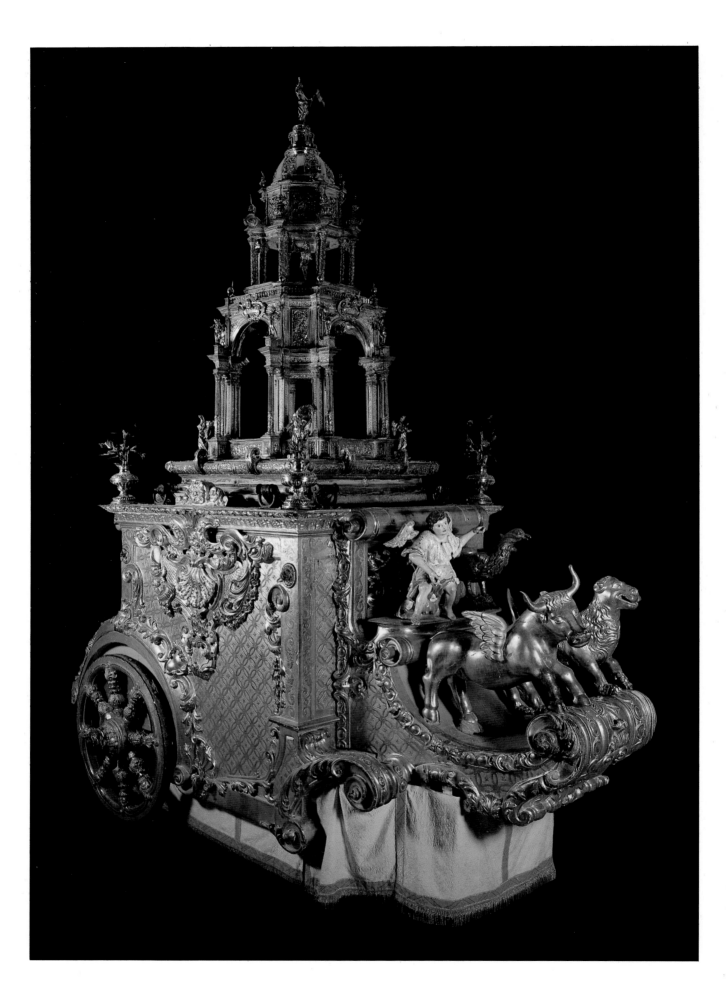

Facing page: *Museum.*
Carriage and processional tabernacle. The carriage was possibly made by Pedro de Riezgo around 1740, and the tabernacle was made by the Madrid goldsmith Rafael González, who worked on it from 1563 to 1567. It is taken round the streets of Segovia to celebrate Corpus Christi.

Top: *Among the few paintings preserved in the cathedral, this Madonna is worthy of mention. It is a Flemish painting on board from the circle of Van Orley. 16th Century.*

Bottom: *Charles V and St Francis of Borgia at Yuste. This canvass by Carlos María Esquivel is the only historical painting in the cathedral. It is dated 1862.*

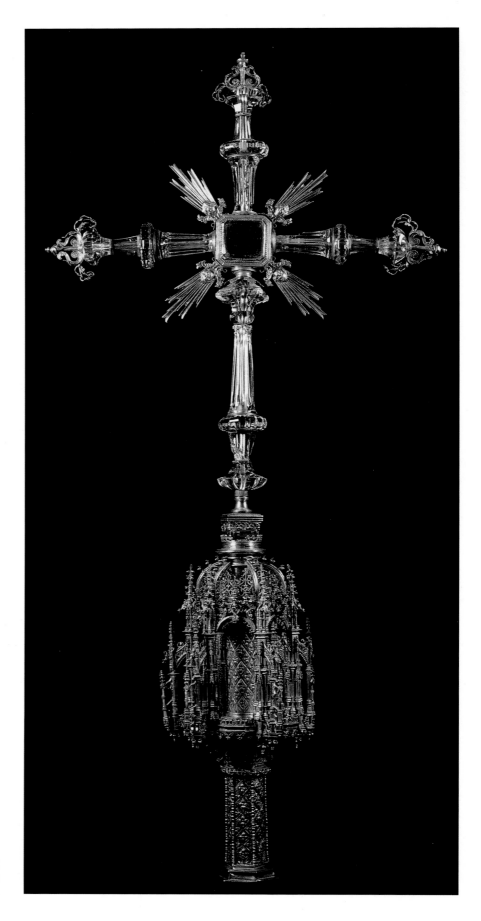

Museum. Silver-gilt and rock crystal processional cross. This singular piece was wrought by the local silversmith Antonio de Oquendo in 1519.

to be steered by the four evangelists in their symbolic form, the Tetramorph. It may have been made by Pedro de Riezgo around 1740-45, and it was gilded by Santiago Casado, who did other pieces in the cathedral.

A staircase made in 1555 and with its handrail adorned with a Tetramorph carved by Jerome of Antwerp takes us to the upper floor, or library. The stairwell is hung with ten large tapestries and two small ones. The largest is of the Story of Zenobia, which we have already seen; three with the monogram B.B. and the names Cristiaen van Bruston and Bernart van Bruston are of the story of Pompey the Great, and the rest, monogrammed B.B.I(acob) V(on) Z(ennen), depict mythological gods.

In the room used until a few years ago for files, various objects are on show on the neo-Gothic shelves. Inside the door, from left to right, is a canvass by Maella (Madonna and Child, 18th Century). In the glass cases are several engravings and watercolours of Segovia's past, among them one by Ricardo de Madrazo of St Andrew's Gate, and coins from the Segovia mint. The best pieces are the silver-gilt and rock crystal Processional Cross, a masterpiece by the Segovian Antonio de Oquendo, dated 1519 and a panel of the Madonna and Child from the circle of Van Orley. Among the items on display opposite are two sets of vestments, the first having belonged to Bishop Juan Arias Dávila, with his arms (eagle, castle and cross) amid Renaissance decoration, an early example of the use of this style in Segovia, and the second to Bishop Fadrique of Portugal, from the beginning of the 16th Century.

Library.
It was built under the direction of García de Cubillas in the mid 16th Century. The vault bosses are by Master Jerome of Antwerp.

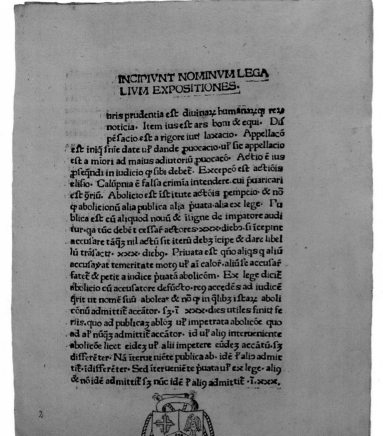

Archives.
Among the bibliographical jewels cherished by the cathedral is Expositiones Nominum Legalium, *printed by Johannes Parix, held to be the first book to be printed in Spain.*

The display is completed with reliquaries, cloths, documents and books, among them the very popular and interesting *Crónica Mundi*, one of the first to be illustrated with engravings.

Back in the cloister, and continuing the walk rightwards, next to the door is the little chapel of Canon López Aguado, who died in 1529. It is attributed to the disciples of Vasco de la Zarza and is one of Segovia's earliest Renaissance pieces.

Next, at the top of the wall, is a naïve 18th-Century representation of the miracle of Marisaltos*, the Jewish woman who, pushed off a cliff for adultery, arrived safely at the bottom by the intercession of the Blessed Virgin. The story was told by Alfonso the Wise in the *Cantigas***. The present painting is a coarse repainting of the original made in 1561 by Alonso de Arévalo.

Further along is the 15th-Century Gothic chapel of Cabrera (?), brought here from its previous site together with the cloister, and by the way out is the cenotaph of Bishop Luis Tello Maldonado, who died in 1581, made by Rodrigo del Solar. The image of Our Lady of Mercy came from the demolished convent of the same name.

* The reference is to Esther, a Segovian Jewess of the 13th Century, who, after the miracle, took the name María del Salto ("Mary of the Jump"), to become known popularly as "Marisaltos" - *translator's note.*

** Medieval songs and poems - *translator's note.*

BIBLIOGRAPHY

AA.VV. *Las Catedrales de Castilla y León*. Edilesa. León, 1992.

CASASECA CASASECA, Antonio. Trazas para la catedral de Segovia. *Archivo Español de Arte*. 1978.

CONTRERAS Y LOPEZ DE AYALA, J. de. La Capilla Mayor de la Catedral. *Estudios Segovianos,* IV, 12, 1952, pp. 521-525.

CONTRERAS Y LOPEZ DE AYALA, J. de. Las vidrieras "Quinientistas" de la catedral de Segovia". *Archivo Español de Arte*, 87, 1949, pp. 193-206.

CORTON DE LAS HERAS, María Teresa. *La construcción de la catedral de Segovia*. Universidad Complutense. Madrid, 1990.

HERNANDEZ OTERO, Arturo. Juan Guas. Maestro de obras de la catedral de Segovia. *Boletín del Seminario de Estudios de Arte y Arqueología*. Valladolid, 1946.

LLAGUNO Y AMIROLA, E. Memoria del canónigo de Segovia Juan Rodríguez... *Noticias de los arquitectos y arquitectura de España desde su restauración*. I. ed. fac. Madrid, 1977, pp. 325-340.

CORTON DE LAS HERAS, María Teresa. *La construcción de la catedral de Segovia*. Universidad Complutense. Madrid, 1990.

QUADRADO, José María. *España. Sus monumentos y artes. Su naturaleza e historia*. Barcelona, 1884.

RUIZ HERNANDO, José Antonio. La Catedral de Segovia. *Las Catedrales de Castilla y León*. I. Avila, 1994.

SANZ Y SANZ, Hilario. Bosquejo histórico de dos catedrales. *Estudios Segovianos,* XIX, 56-57, 1967, pp. 161-204.

VILLALPANDO, Manuela. *Origen y construcción de la catedral de Segovia*. *Estudios Segovianos*, XIV, 42, 1962, pp. 391-408.

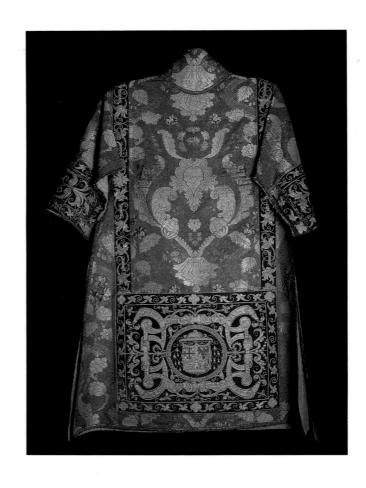

Dalmatic of Bishop Juan Arias Dávila.
Don Juan Arias Dávila, of Converso *origin (converted from Judaism -*
translator's note)*, was one of the most cultivated men in 15th-Century*
Segovia. His loathing for Isabel the Catholic brought about his death
in Rome in 1497.
The dalmatic, which he donated to the cathedral, is of the greatest interest, as
it is one of the earliest local Renaissance pieces. The family arms - eagle,
castle and cross - gave rise to satirical antisemitic rhymes.